E V E R W O V E N

EVERWOVEN

A Memoir.
A Reckoning.

Megan Margherio

2025

Published by Everwoven Publishing

First edition: 2025

ISBNs:
Paperback: 979-8-9988134-0-5
Hardcover: 979-8-9988134-1-2
eBook: 979-8-9988134-2-9
Audiobook: 979-8-9988134-3-6

Library of Congress Control Number: 2025916391
(This book has been submitted to the Library of Congress for cataloging.)

Cover art by Varsam Kurnia
Copy editing by Andie Woodard
Proofreading by Trinity McFadden

This book is a work of creative nonfiction.
While grounded in the author's lived experiences, names and identifying
details have been changed or omitted to honor privacy and emotional truth.
Some dialogue has been reconstructed for clarity and narrative flow.

For more information, visit www.meganmargherio.com

Printed in the United States of America

For Me.

For every version of myself—past, present, and future—who endured, who dreamed, who doubted, who dared.

For the little girl who didn't yet have the words, the teenager who raged and wept, the young woman who kept getting back up, the woman who chose to heal, the woman I am now who stands in her own light, and the woman I am still becoming.

This is for us. We are the threads that wove this story into being—together.

And for My Bright Spots.

For much of my life, the shadows in my mind were my world. Their shapes on the walls of my memories were my only truth. But even when I felt alone in the darkness, there were those who held out a candle—a flicker of light that shifted the shadows, made them take up less space, even if it was only for a moment.

These candles helped my eyes learn to bear the light. My light.

This page is for them—my bright spots. Thank you for showing me that my light was safe—and that even when I was stumbling in the dark, I was never truly walking alone.

- -

Jason	Brandi	Robyn	Meghan
Carter	Tamara	Marilyn	Lena
Robynn	Barzin	Sarah H.	Rachel
Scott T.	Andrew	Krista	Rianna
Jim M.	Anderson	Staci	Alka
Becky M.	Stephen	Doris	Cassie
Josh	Van	Wilbur	Jim D.
Andrea	Katherine	Michelle P.	Michael
Justin	Sean	Ashley	Annie
Sarah M.	Sheri	Scott S.	Morgan
Tara	Matt K.	Taryn	Keith
Bob	Peggy	Yann	Michelle S.
Linda	Chris H.	Anna	Siobhan
Doug	Frankie	Inga	
Becky E.	Dawn	Chris B.	*Every former*
Amanda	Sharon	Edward	*student of mine*
Brittni	Milena	Sebastian	

- -

AUTHOR'S NOTE

What follows is a memoir, but not in the traditional sense. *Everwoven* is not a chronological retelling of my life. Rather, it is a reckoning, a conversation between the past versions of myself and the present. From the beginning, this book was designed as a space to honor those versions—the ones I silenced, ignored, and tried to erase. In my trauma healing, I have been working to reclaim my voice, but to do that, I needed to let all of me—every past version—speak. *Everwoven* is the result of that work.

Everything you read on the following pages is my truth, my reclamation, but I intentionally crafted this story to allow you to *feel*, rather than simply *observe*, what happened. This is a deeply vulnerable work. I am inviting you into my mind, my healing work, and my experiences. I do not sanitize my truth.

Throughout the story, you will encounter many vignettes—short, fragmented moments in my life. These are memories in their purest form: The version of me who lived them dictated those moments into my phone from the floor of my closet. The vignettes remain almost entirely verbatim to preserve their authenticity and the voice of my past self. It was critical that each version of me told their story in their words. This is how I chose to honor them.

My past versions are not characters. They are all me—different, yet connected.

At the beginning and end of each chapter, you'll find direct conversations between my past and present selves—my inner healing work on display. *Everwoven* takes place entirely in my mind, which is why its structure differs from a traditional memoir. You may notice an absence of detailed scene-setting. That's intentional. I want to keep you inside the emotional world of each past self—not outside it, observing. More description would only create distance from the raw emotional truth.

Throughout the book, I refer to past versions of myself as Little Me, Teen Me, 20s Me, and 30s Me rather than giving exact ages. This is intentional. Each version of me represents a time in my life, not a specific year. Trauma distorts time, and memory doesn't always fit into neat, chronological order. These versions of me exist across years, shaped by experiences rather than exact numbers. Their age isn't the focus—their emotions are.

You'll also notice that I do not provide names or descriptions of those who caused my trauma. This, too, was a deliberate choice. By refusing to name them, I reclaim my power. I refuse to center them, acknowledge them, or allow them any more space in my life beyond the harm they caused.

While this is my personal story, the structure is designed to allow readers to see themselves in it. By providing fewer details about places and people, I create space for you to project your own experiences onto the page. We don't need to share the same story to share the same emotions, which is why this is not just my story—it is meant to be a mirror for anyone who has lived through trauma, survival, and healing.

You may also notice short, almost lyrical sentences throughout the book. This is in part to honor my voice as a writer but, more importantly, to reflect how trauma is recounted by survivors: in bursts of blunt, fragmented memories that blur time. As a trauma survivor, my authorial voice naturally follows this rhythm.

Similarly, you might notice repetition of certain words, images, or emotions. These are not oversights. They are emotional echoes, and they are intentional.

Healing rarely moves in straight lines. It loops. It circles back.

Sometimes, we need to touch the same wound from different angles—at different ages, with different hands—before we understand it.

The echoes in this book mirror that process. They reflect how trauma reverberates across time—and how healing, too, must ripple back through what's been buried.

You'll find language that repeats, sensations that return, and moments that echo earlier ones—not as mistakes, but as invitations. These are the places I've had to revisit again and again. This is how I've come to understand healing: not as a single breakthrough, but as a series of quiet recognitions. I've done my best to bring you with me through each one.

This book carries weight. Stories in these pages may press against wounds or feel too familiar, including childhood sexual abuse, suicidal ideation, intimate partner violence, PTSD, self-loathing, and self-blame. As you read, please be aware of your needs and honor yourself. I would rather you stop reading than create unnecessary stress or harm for yourself.

Finally, I ask that you engage with *Everwoven* as it is, rather than through the expectations of what a memoir "should" be. I encourage you to let go of traditional storytelling expectations and allow yourself to *experience* the book, rather than analyze it—because that's what I designed it to be: an immersive experience where our common humanity is reflected back to us. You may not see my exact story, but you may find yourself in its reflection. And in that, I hope you feel less alone.

1.

The Inheritance

"Are you there, Little Me?" I hold my breath, hoping.

Silence.

But I feel her. I know she's there, hovering just beyond my awareness. Watching.

"I know you're there. The air thickens when you're near. I can hear your breath—small, quiet, waiting."

The butterflies pick up their pace in my stomach. My heart flutters. I'm nervous. I take a long breath to calm down before trying a different approach.

"I don't blame you for hiding. I get it now.
I left you behind. I made you carry it all alone.
I see that now. I'm so sorry.
And I want to do better."

A whisper. Sharp. Skeptical. *"You always say that."*

Little Me steps into the light. Her ponytail bounces as she moves, scabbed knees peeking from beneath shorts still too big for her. Hand-me-downs from her sister. A farmer's tan showing the contrast between her pale freckled skin and a life spent outdoors. Her brown eyes are looking down, staring at her muddy sneakers. Her fingers pick at the skin around her nails—twitchy, restless.

She stops fidgeting for the first time, just for a second. *"So, what do you want?"*

It's a fair question. One that deserves an honest answer.

"I don't want anything, Little Me. I'm here because here is where I should have been all along. I messed up before by ignoring you. I was too scared to hear your truth. But I've been working on getting stronger, and I want to be with you now."

She looks up at me, her eyes sharp. *"Why should I believe you?"*

Her eyes test me, searching for the lie. I expected this. I would doubt me, too.

"Because this time, I'm staying. I'm ready to listen.
I finally understand the fear that kept you in the shadows.
The same fear I carry, too—being too much and never enough at the same time."

Her little fingers stop picking at her nails. She knows that fear.

"You've carried it for so long, haven't you?" I ask softly, hoping to put her at ease.

She nods, almost imperceptibly. *"Yeah. I learned it before I even knew what it was. Before I had the words for it. But I knew the feeling. I still do."*

"I do, too," I say, looking down at my feet.

Little Me shifts, hesitating, then lifts her chin. *"I remember the rules that weren't spoken but had to be followed. I remember learning that I could be loved, but only when I was good. That I could be seen, but only when I made her proud. That I could exist, but only on her terms."* She takes a shaky breath. *"Do you remember that?"*

My hands twitch. I press my nails into my skin, trying to ground myself. I could look away, deflect. But I don't. I owe her this.

"I remember."

She narrows her eyes. *"I don't think you do. I think you remember the events, but you don't remember what it felt like to live with her."*

Her voice is stronger now. She stands up straighter, her little feet planting firmly on the ground.

"You said you're here to listen," she says, arms crossing over her chest. *"So prove it. Listen to just a few of my stories. Then let's see if you remember what it was like."*

Bright Spots

I knew how to walk around eggshells. Not the kind that crunched under your feet, but a kind that lived in the air—floating, invisible, always waiting to shatter.

I knew the rules. I knew how to be good. I knew what happened when I wasn't.

Life was supposed to be easier here. It was supposed to be idyllic. And in a lot of ways, it was. It was safe here, at least on the outside.

I lived in a Midwestern town with just 55 people. No stoplight. No gas station. No store. No business of any kind, really. Just farms. A neighboring Amish community (more farms). A three-room school. Two churches. One where the old people went. The other church had a preacher who handled snakes. I think it was Pentecostal.

I got baptized there before we started going to another church in a nearby town.

My town was the kind of place where everyone knew everyone and everything about everyone. I had known the same people since I was born. I knew their kids. I knew their parents. I knew who farmed soybeans and who farmed wheat. People there were grateful for what they had. They did what they could for others because it was the right thing to do.

My school was no exception. Teachers took on extra roles to make sure all 30 of us in grades K–8 had as many opportunities as kids in bigger schools.

My PE teacher was also the principal. She had a paddle mounted on the wall behind her desk, so I didn't like to go near there.

Our school cook, Jane, was also a custodian. She made special lunches for every kid in school on their birthday, which was one of my favorite things. I spent a lot of time thinking about what I wanted my birthday lunch to be, even though I always chose the same thing—porcupine meatballs, mashed potatoes, peas, and a chocolate chip cookie.

Our bus driver, Marilyn, was also a custodian. She was the mother of one of my friends. She was a safe person for me. I never told her anything. But I knew she was safe.

In so many ways, life in that tiny town was magical.

I played outside a lot, riding bikes with my friends Krista and Staci.

We knew every inch of the gravel roads around our houses. We could find the quickest path to anywhere.

We had sleepovers at each other's houses. There was always something fun to do.

At Staci's, we jumped on the trampoline and practiced gymnastics routines.

At Krista's, we played in her barn. Her mom sometimes made Swedish pancakes when I stayed over because she knew I liked them.

My town came together for a lot of community events, almost always at the school.

Back-to-school picnics. Spaghetti suppers. Chili nights.

When we had our Christmas pageants, we hosted them at the old people's church. We needed the extra space. The entire community showed up. They cared about the school. They cared about the kids.

But my favorite example of that happened in first grade.

Grandparents Day was coming, and I didn't have anyone to bring. My grandmothers were still alive, but they lived on opposite sides of the state. One couldn't drive. The other couldn't afford to make the trip.

I thought I was going to be left out.

I acted like it wasn't a big deal, even though it was.

That year, the Carpenters decided to adopt me for the day.

They weren't my real grandparents, but they didn't seem to care. They just showed up. Like they belonged there.

Like I belonged there.

Even as I got older, they kept coming for Grandparents Day.

They took pictures with me.

They ate lunch with me.

We played games together.

It meant a lot that they always showed up. So, every year, I gave them my newest school picture. I wanted them to know I appreciated their kindness.

One summer, Krista and I were swimming in the Carpenter's pond when Doris invited me inside.

She wanted to show me something.

She had my most recent school picture on their wall.

Right next to their real grandkids.

I felt the blood rush to my face. At first, I was embarrassed. Then, I started to tear up.

I still don't know why it meant so much to me that they put my picture on their wall.

But it did.

Maybe because it was one of the only times someone chose me.

The Carpenters were bright spots for me. They were reminders of the good in the world.

When I thought about them, I felt warm. Safe. Happy.

They were teaching me what kind of person I wanted to be when I got older.

The Carpenters were good people for the sake of being good people. Never expecting anything in return.

I wanted to be like that.

The Carpenters showed me what love looked like.

But at home, love looked different.

It came with rules.

Rules no one said out loud.

But I learned them quickly.

Unspoken Rules

At home, there were rules for chores.

I was supposed to clean my room once a week. I was messy, so this was always a challenge for me.

I was supposed to put the dishes away and refill the dishwasher every day. I got pretty good at loading it, but my stepfather still had to remind me—some of the forks went in tongs first, some went in handle first, so they didn't stick together.

I never understood why that was so hard to remember.

Those were the spoken rules.

But there were others.

No one wrote them down.

No one said them out loud.

But they weren't the kind of rules you could forget.

Rule #1: Love had conditions.

If I did well, my mother bragged about me.
If I failed, I disappeared.

Rule #2: I was responsible for her emotions.

If she was in a good mood, I was safe.
If she wasn't, I braced myself.

Rule #3: The mask had to stay on.

My mother was a wonderful mother.
We were a perfect family.
No one could ever know otherwise.

I was good at following rules. I prided myself on that.

I was good at making sure she stayed happy.

But sometimes, I failed.

The Spelling Test

In second grade, I brought home a spelling test.

Nine out of 10 correct.

Even the challenge words.

I was proud of myself.

I showed it to my mother.

She barely looked at me.

She set the paper down. Walked into the living room.

Turned on *Days of Our Lives*.

The episode she had recorded.

I followed her. Tried to say something.

She turned up the volume.

Louder.

Loud enough to drown me out.

I hung my head in shame.

I knew I had messed up.

Now it was time for my punishment.

She wouldn't speak to me for a week.

That night, I thought about it over and over.

Tracing the letters of the word I had misspelled with my finger under my blanket.

I whispered it to myself until it didn't even sound like a word anymore.

D-E-F-I-N-I-T-E-L-Y.

I made a promise to myself.

Next time, I'd get it right.

Next time, she wouldn't have a reason to ignore me.

The following Friday, I took another test.

More challenge words.

This time, I got 100 percent.

That night, the silence lifted.

My mother started talking to me again.

She acted as if nothing had happened.

And everything went back to normal.

I didn't cry.

I didn't ask why she ignored me.

I understood the lesson:

Love could be taken away.

Perfection was the expectation.

And I wouldn't make that mistake again.

The Mask

On the outside, we looked like a loving family.

My mother was on the school board.

She sewed my costumes for school plays and Christmas pageants.

She showed up to every event, smiling. Proud.

From the outside looking in, my mother was a good mother.

I knew it was all fake. But I always hoped—maybe if she pretended hard enough, it would become true.

I watched her.

Without saying a word, she showed me how to pretend, too. She showed me how to be the daughter she wanted. She showed me what happened when I wasn't.

I don't even know when I realized—

to survive her, I had to abandon myself.

It happened slowly.

One piece at a time.

I let go of anything that disappointed her.

Anything that made her angry.

I followed all of her rules.

Because I didn't want to feel invisible again.

That was the cruelest punishment of all.

Not the yelling. Not the insults. Not the silence.

But the moment she decided I didn't exist.

And she did it so easily.

The Playground Fall

I was six when I first learned love could be taken away.

It happened during a school chili supper.

I was on the playground. Climbing. Running. Laughing.

I was playing with my friends.

It was fun.

And then—

I fell.

I hit the ground so hard, all the air left my body.

I tried to inhale, but nothing came.

My stomach hurt.

The world spun.

I didn't know if I had hit my head or not.

I got scared.

I started to panic.

Before I could find my voice to stop them, my friends ran. To get my mother. My stepfather. Someone.

My stepfather came first.

He bent down.

Dusted me off.

Made sure I could breathe.

Then he walked away.

Back inside.

Minutes passed.

I was still trying to take a deep breath without my stomach hurting when my mother appeared.

For a second, I thought maybe—

maybe she came because she was worried.

Maybe she was going to hug me.

Rub my back.

Tell me I was okay.

Instead, she pulled me aside.

Lowered her voice.

"Your clumsiness is embarrassing. People were worried you could have really hurt yourself."

I felt my face flush.

Shame burned through me.

Like fire ants crawling under my skin.

I wanted to tell her I couldn't breathe. That I was scared.

But I already knew the rule.

This was not a place for my feelings.

This was a place for protecting hers.

I looked down. Shuffled my feet in the mulch.

"Wipe your face off and get inside. Show everyone you're fine, so I don't look like I raised a little baby."

I swallowed everything.

The fear. The pain. The hope—

that maybe this time, she would have been different.

I stood up.

Pulled some mulch from my hair.

I walked back inside. Into each of the three classrooms.

So everyone could see—

I was fine.

I pretended nothing had happened.

Because that was the rule.

She was mad at me after the chili supper.

My stepfather stuck up for me, but it didn't matter.

I had already messed up.

I embarrassed her.

All that remained was my punishment.

She pretended I didn't exist for two days.

That was how it always was with her.

If I cried, I was weak.
If I was happy, I was annoying.
If I was too loud, I was obnoxious.
If I was too quiet, I was sulking.

No matter what I did—
I was always too much.

And never enough.

At the exact same time.

- -

Little Me stops talking. I can tell she's fighting back tears.

"Do you remember what it was like now?"

Her voice is sad and heavy.

I can tell it's hard for her to go back to these feelings of inadequacy and rejection.

I wait to make sure she's done speaking. Her eyes are locked on mine. She's waiting for me.

"I remember." I nod slowly. My lips curl downward.

"I know how carefully you walked the tightrope of our mother's emotions. I hear you when you talk about having to erase yourself, little by little, to keep her comfortable. You worked so hard to never be a burden to her, but it didn't work."

Little Me breaks eye contact.

She shuffles her feet.

I continue, "I hear your quiet, aching hope that one day, she might love you differently. And I hear the silence she gave you instead."

I bend down, grabbing Little Me's hand.

She looks up at me, still blinking back tears.

"That feeling of being too much and never enough at the same time?

It's still here.

It's why I still second-guess myself. Even on the little stuff.
It's why I hesitate before I speak, making sure my words don't take
up
too
much
space.

It's why I read a room before I let bigger parts of my personality show.

It's why I still feel like if I am too much, I'll be a problem—

and if I do too little, I'll be a disappointment."

I shake my head and let out a deep sigh.

"I still feel it all, and I'm still undoing her lie."

A tear slides down Little Me's cheek.

I reach out, wiping it away.

She sniffs. Her little voice is barely above a whisper.

*"If it's a lie, why did she do it? Did she want me to feel that way? Did she want
to hurt me?"*

"Little Me, you were just a child who wanted to be seen,
to be loved, to belong.

That is not a crime.

That is what is supposed to come with being in a family.
It's why you know it wasn't okay. You knew
you were supposed to be loved.
She just couldn't give it to you."

I pause, looking into her sad face. The brown freckles on her tiny nose. The scars on her brow. One from a dog bite. The other from a car accident.

"I don't know if she wanted you to feel that way.

And the thing is, we don't get to know.

That's for her to carry, and it's something she still refuses to face."

I look into her heavy brown eyes. She looks right back at me.

"But it's not your fault, Little Me.

You didn't do anything wrong."

Little Me starts to chew on her lip.

"Little Me, I need you to hear something. Something someone should have told you long ago."

Her eyes widen slightly. Waiting. Almost fearful of what is coming next.

"You were never the problem.

You were never too much.

You were always enough.

Just because she couldn't see it doesn't make it any less true."

She steps back slightly. Scans my face for the lie. Begins scratching at her thumbnails.

"Then why did you leave me? Why was I too much for you?"

I swallow. My throat is dry and scratchy.

"You were never too much for me, Little Me.

I didn't feel like I was enough for you.

I was ashamed of myself for abandoning you,

so I tried to pretend I hadn't.

It was wrong.

And I am sorry.

You deserved better."

Little Me pulls her hand back slightly. Her young face has skepticism written all over it.

"How do I know you're telling the truth right now?"

"It's okay if you don't believe me yet, Little Me.
I know I taught you that I would leave.

But this time is different.

I am strong enough to stand in the truth for both of us."

Little Me crosses her arms. Her nose wrinkles as she studies me. Like she's trying to decide if I'm safe. If I really mean it.

I keep my voice steady.

"I don't know if you fully realize what you did that was so amazing, Little Me."

She stares at me. She's not used to compliments.

"Because you held onto love, I can love myself now.

Because you never let go of hope, I am standing here today.

Because you refused to let the world steal your light,
I still have one inside of me.

You held onto what makes us magical.

You saved me without even realizing it."

Little Me shifts uncomfortably, her hands twisting the hem of her shirt. I can tell I'm starting to make her uneasy with these truths about who she really is.

She sniffs again, wiping her nose on her sleeve.

Her voice is softer this time.

"How do I know you won't leave again?"

I freeze.

She doesn't ask with anger. She asks because she needs to know. Because she's still bracing for me to disappear. Because I've done it before.

"Little Me, even when I couldn't look at you,
even when I pushed you away,
even when I ignored you because I wasn't strong enough to face you,
you protected the best parts of me. And I owe you everything."

She looks away only for a second before bringing her eyes back to meet mine.

"So, no, I won't leave.

Not this time.

Not ever again.

Because even if the world never sees you for the magical human you are—

I do."

A tear slips from her jaw, falling onto her shoe.

I smile slightly. I reach for her hand.

"And here's the thing:
For the first time,

I love what I see."

Little Me lets go of my hand.

And then she throws herself into my arms.

Her tiny body collapses against me. A flood of tears spills down her face as she clings to me.

Her breath is ragged. Her body shakes.

Like she's afraid I'll disappear. Like if she doesn't hold on tight enough, I'll slip back into the shadows.

I hug her close.

Rub her back.

"You're going to be okay," I whisper.
"I'm here with you.
And I'm not going anywhere."

2.

The Deadbolt Years

I feel her before I see her.

She isn't hesitant. She doesn't wait.

She's already here.

She has been waiting for this—not because she needs me but because she wants me to suffer.

She steps forward, a scowl on her face.

I can already tell.

Teen Me wants justice. She wants me to feel what she felt. To sit in the silence she was left in. She wants me to taste the bitterness of her loneliness.

She shifts her weight onto one leg, arms crossed, a blank expression on her face.

She studies me. Calculating. Deciding how she's going to make me pay for abandoning her.

Her voice is cold, but there's a flicker of amusement beneath it.

"Oh, great. You."

She tilts her head, looking at me like I'm a bad joke. Like she already knows how this will go. Like she's bored before we've even begun.

She exhales through her nose. Slow. Measured. Calculating.

Her eyes never leave mine.

I swallow.

I can tell this won't be easy.

She's the one I am the most afraid of. She's the one who needed me the most. And every time she tried to get my attention, I shoved her back into the recesses of my mind and pretended I couldn't hear her calling for me.

Anything to avoid confronting the pain she carries.

I force myself to hold steady. "You sound angry."

Her lip curls. Almost amused.

"Oh my God. Are you serious?"

She tilts her head, like she's just been handed a gift. Like she expected me to be boring, predictable—pathetic. And I just handed it to her on a silver fucking platter.

"That's adorable. 'You sound angry.'"

She mimics my tone, exaggerating her voice into something ridiculous.

"Wow. Amazing insight. You're really digging deep today, huh?"

I exhale. I know what she's doing. She's baiting me.

She wants me to get frustrated. Defensive. She wants to see if I'll fight her—or if I'll do what everyone else did to her.

Shut down. Walk away. Leave her to handle it on her own.

I don't move. I don't react.

I just let her have the space to push me further.

She knows she's in control and lets the silence stretch.

Her eyes never waver. I don't think she even blinks. She just stares at me like she's looking through me.

Then she smiles. But it's not a real smile.

It's a blade.

"Alright. Let's play your stupid game. You get to be the grown-up, and I'll be the poor, broken girl you ignored for decades. You can say some stupid therapy bullshit that makes you feel better, and you'll disappear— and I will go right back to being alone."

She steps forward, slow and deliberate.

She uncrosses her arms. Her eyes lock onto mine.

She's gearing up.

For what, I don't know. But my gut tells me, *Get ready for anything.*

"You're here to heal me, right? That's what you want?"

"No—"

"Right, right, sorry, I forgot. You're here to listen. You're here to hold space for me and my pain."

She laughs, rolling her eyes.

I feel her bitterness in my ribs. It's searing.

She's trying to hurt me. Trying to punish me.

I don't stand up to her. I don't correct her.

Because I know what she's doing. And there's a part of me that believes I deserve it.

"You want to talk about my emotions? That's funny. Because when I actually needed you, you didn't have anything to offer. You just left me to wither under the weight of what I went through."

Her words are calm. Casual.

Not a single ounce of vulnerability slips through. Just facts.

And somehow, that makes them land even harder.

"You erased me. And now you're here, pretending like you give a shit?"

She doesn't budge. Doesn't even lean in.

She just waits.

Not hoping I'll say something different. Just waiting for confirmation that I won't.

I want to tell her she's wrong. I want to tell her I never stopped caring.

But that's not true.

"I'm not here to rewrite history, Teen Me."

(Silence.)

"I'm here because I finally understand the fear that's been driving you. The fear of having to do it all alone."

She starts to shuffle her feet.

For a brief second, I think I have her.

I'm wrong.

"You know what's hilarious?"

She tilts her head. A viper ready to strike.

She gives me a moment—as if she expects me to respond.

I don't.

She smirks. She can feel my uneasiness.

And she's enjoying it.

"I actually thought things would get better when Robynn moved out."

She lets out a dry, humorless laugh.

"Like, what kind of idiot would believe that? Seriously."

She shakes her head.

"As if suddenly my mother was going to wake up one day and realize—Oh, wait! I do have another daughter! I have another chance to be a decent fucking human to someone I am supposed to care about! I actually thought she'd try harder to be a mother to me."

She lets out an enormous sigh.

"God, I was pathetic. No wonder Robynn left as soon as she could and didn't come around much. She saw our mother for who she really was and wanted to get the fuck away. But my dumbass kept hoping for the best."

Her voice is sharp. Biting.

But not at me.

At herself.

She looks at the ground, briefly hanging her head in resignation.

"What a joke. What an absolute fucking joke."

Shaking her head, she sighs. Rolls her shoulders back.

The wall is going back up.

Her emotional armor is thick. Invisible.

But I can feel it.

Its weight is heavy. Familiar.

I stand there, wanting to cry.

Because I know what that armor cost her.

And it was a price too heavy for someone so young.

I try to think of what I can say to let her know she's safe. To let her know the armor can come down.

But she's already onto me.

She's been watching me. Studying me.

She knows I'm searching for something—anything I can use to get through to her.

"You think you're tough enough to withstand my truth? C'mon. You've been run-ning from me for years. What's so different now?"

Her eyebrow lifts. She thinks she has me against the ropes.

"Teen Me, you don't see it yet, but I am not the same person who ran from you all those years ago. I am stronger now. More able to hold my truth—all of it. That means holding your truth, too."

She stares at me.

"I'm not going anywhere. I am here for your truth. All of it. Even the ugliest parts."

Silence.

Then—

"Fine. If you think you're strong enough to handle my story—let's see what you've got."

The Lie

I thought maybe—just maybe—things would be different.

That maybe, if I was the only one left, she would finally notice me. Maybe, if I was quiet enough, good enough, small enough, she would soften. Maybe, if I didn't make her life harder, she would finally see me. Maybe she would finally be glad she had me.

But almost nothing changed when Robynn moved out.

The house was quieter without my sister constantly complaining about how annoying I was.

Without her making fun of me for being a nerd.

But the rest of it?

It stayed the same.

My mother still belittled me. She still treated me like an inconvenience. Acted like I wasn't even there. Used her love as a weapon.

During this time, she told me how hard she fought to have me.

How she was in the ICU while pregnant with me. How the doctors had to give her a bunch of medications just to keep her alive. How they had to be careful about which ones they used.

She told me the doctors said the medications that would help her the most—would likely terminate her pregnancy.

She said she didn't want to do that. So she was sicker than she had to be. In the hospital longer.

Shortly after telling me this story, she got mad at me.

For not cleaning my room well enough.

I tried to argue with her.

And she reacted.

It was the first time she told me—she should have listened to the doctors. She should have taken the better medications.

It wouldn't be the last.

And then—after a few short months of being an only child—my mother and stepfather told me we were fostering a boy. He was the same age as me.

A kid who had a hard life. A kid they wanted to make things easier for.

They turned the laundry room into his bedroom.

Because my mother didn't want to give up the office she had after my sister moved out.

Within weeks, the washer and dryer moved into the dining room. They painted the walls of the laundry room blue. They bought a trundle bed.

Boys clothes hung in a new closet. The air still smelled like drywall putty.

They didn't ask me if I wanted this. I wasn't asked how I felt about getting a foster *brother*.

I was just told, "This will be good for everyone."

And because I was still a fucking idiot back then—

I believed them.

Toughen Up

It started off fine.

He was quiet at first.

My mother said it might take him time to feel like part of the family.

We played basketball in the backyard, the hoop mounted on a great big walnut tree.

He tossed walnuts at me when I tried to shoot the ball.

I laughed it off.

We watched *The Simpsons* and *Animaniacs* after school. Acted out silly stories with his Teenage Mutant Ninja Turtles action figures and my Barbies.

But there was something about the way he watched me.

Something that made me uneasy, even though I couldn't explain why.

Then he kicked me in the stomach while we were playing.

I thought it was an accident.

He never said anything when I groaned. Never apologized.

The second time, I thought I had done something to piss him off.

We were playing freeze tag with Staci and another girl.

He tagged me.

I froze like I was supposed to.

Then he threw me to the ground. Kicked me so hard, I had bruises on my stomach.

I told my mother what happened. Showed her the outlines of the bruises still forming.

She barely looked.

"Boys play differently," she said. "They're more aggressive. If you're going to keep playing with him, you'll need to toughen up."

The third time, I knew the truth.

I was on my own.

She was going to excuse him. To protect him. To blame me.

No matter what.

And once I realized that—

things got way fucking easier.

I stopped reacting when he broke my toys in front of me. I stopped crying when he said my parents didn't want me. I stopped expecting my mother to care. I stopped bothering to tell anyone.

No one was coming for me.

I was on my own.

I thought, *If I let things roll off my back, let them pass through me—that means I'm tough.*

If I didn't cry, if I didn't get angry, if I didn't scream or react—maybe I would finally be safe.

It didn't work. My so-called *brother* kept finding ways to beat me up.

And that's when I realized—maybe losing parts of myself was a good thing.

If I didn't get attached to things—I wouldn't have to feel the loss when they were taken.

If I didn't let myself want love—I wouldn't have to feel the pain of being denied it.

If I stopped feeling entirely—I wouldn't have to know how much this was destroying me.

Trundle

They sent him to therapy after he hurt my mother's iguana.

He held a match—
or maybe it was a lighter—
up to the iguana's skin.

It left burn marks.

My mother said it was just a phase. "Boys will be boys."

His adoption was almost final. The state wanted everything to be right.

But they disagreed with my mother.

His case worker said he had to go to weekly sessions with a child psychologist.

At first, I had to go with them, but I didn't meet with the psychologist.

I sat in the waiting room.

Played with the toys in the blue chest. Flipped through *Highlights* magazines. Lost myself in the Hidden Pictures puzzles.

I loved those puzzles. Loved how there was always a solution. A right answer. Something that could be found.

It wasn't long before my mother let me stay home when he had his sessions.

And at one of those sessions—the therapist had my mother call home.

She told my stepfather to look under his bed.

Nothing under the mattress.

She told him to check the trundle.

That's when we found them.

Dozens of them.

Drawings.

All of me.

Dead.

My eyes? Blacked out.

My hair? Bloodied.

Stick figures at my funeral.

And in every. Single. One.

He was smiling.

And next to the drawings—a kitchen knife.

My stomach dropped.

I was right.

It wasn't just in my mind.

I was in danger.

False Safety

That night, he came home from his session like normal. No cops came by. My parents said his drawings were just a fantasy. Nothing to be afraid of.

The next day, my stepfather installed a deadbolt lock on my bedroom door. He turned to me as he tightened the last screw.

"There. Now you're safe."

Safe.

I was supposed to run inside after school and lock myself in. Stay there until my stepfather got home. Believe this was enough.

The deadbolt wasn't for keeping him out.

It was for keeping me in.

I followed the rules.

He got the whole house to himself.

I became a prisoner in my own home.

And he still found ways to get to me.

The pool was the easiest.

We had an above-ground pool, and in the summers I basically lived in it. My auburn hair would turn blonde from the sun and chlorine.

We played games in the pool—*Shark, Marco Polo.*

Sometimes, it was fun.

Other times, it was scary.

He could do whatever he wanted under the water.

He could grab me, and no one would see.

The first time, I thought I was imagining it. His hand ran across the outside of my bikini bottoms, briefly lingering where no one was allowed.

The second time, I knew it was real. A couple of weeks had gone by since the first incident, and I was staying alert but still playing with him. We were playing *Shark*, and he grabbed my legs as I swam away from him.

He held onto my legs, pulling my bikini bottoms off while I squirmed to get away.

He held them in his hand as he put his goggles on. He stuck his head under the water, staring at my body.

He told me he'd give my bikini bottoms back when I stopped covering myself.

I just had to move my hands.

So, I did.

But he didn't give them back.

He grabbed me instead.

Like my body was his for the taking.

I told my mother what he did. Where he put his hands. That I was scared of him.

She didn't believe me.

She told me to stop making up stories for attention.

She told me there were real people experiencing the things I was describing.

I shouldn't make things like that up.

The third time he grabbed me, I stopped swimming in our backyard pool.

The other stuff happened at night.

When my parents were watching TV.

Sometimes, he would just stand outside my bedroom.

I could hear him breathing through the door.

Sometimes, he got in.

I was in my room, reading with the door open so the dog could come lay with me. My parents were in the living room.

He came out of the bathroom. Walked past my door wearing a towel.

Then walked back by, exposing his fully erect penis in my doorway.

I told my stepfather.

He said he'd take care of it.

A few days later, I was sitting on my bed, drawing. My door was closed, but it wasn't locked.

The next thing I remember, I was lying on my back.

He was holding me down.

I tried to get away, but he was stronger than me.

He started rubbing his erection against my leg.

Panic surged through my body.

I screamed for my stepfather. The weight on top of me vanished.

He ran back into the bathroom.

I locked my deadbolt.

My stepfather never came.

He couldn't hear me over the TV.

I sat on the floor, my legs trembling, my heart racing.

I started hyperventilating.

I puked all over my purple carpet.

I watched the yellow bile mix with the fibers.

I felt just as dirty as my carpet.

I sat there, staring into nothingness.

Eventually, I got up, steadied my legs, and went to tell my parents I got sick. My mother got annoyed about cleaning up the puke.

I didn't even bother telling them what happened.

I just disconnected.

From my body.

From my mind.

From everything.

A Stranger and Danger

The moment I knew I was in danger wasn't when he kicked me or taunted me.

Though it should have been.

It wasn't even when he started doing worse things to me.

It was at a resort. In a pool. With people everywhere.

We were playing tag, dunking each other in the deeper water.

It was a game.

Until it wasn't.

He held me under.

At first, I thought he would let go.

But he didn't let go.

I squirmed. Kicked. Fought.

I panicked, desperately trying to get away from him.

The harder I squirmed, the harder he held me down. My lungs burned. My body started to slow.

He still didn't let go.

I don't know how long I was under, but it was long enough that a stranger—another mother—screamed at him to stop.

When I surfaced, coughing and gasping for air, she called me to her.

He swam to the ladder and got out of the pool.

She kept calling for me to come to her.

I swam to the ledge where she was standing. I was still coughing up pool water.

She rubbed my back. She asked if I was okay. She asked who he was to me.

And for the first time, someone saw a piece of what I had been living through.

For the first time, someone believed me before I even said a word.

I left the pool after a bit. I went to find my mother. I thought maybe, finally, this time, she would protect me.

But she had already spoken to him first.

When I got back to our camper, she was waiting for me.

He was already inside.

She looked disgusted with me.

I tried to tell her what happened.

She stopped me before I could.

"Your dramatic behavior is why that mother got involved. You should apologize. He didn't deserve to be embarrassed like that. He had to leave the pool because he was so uncomfortable."

That's when I knew.

I was alone in this.

I stopped asking for help.

Instead, I started asking myself: *What am I doing wrong? Why do I keep making him mad? How do I fix this?*

I stopped fighting him. I started watching him. I adapted.

I made myself smaller.

Because if no one was coming to save me, I had to learn how to survive on my own.

I just had to keep surviving. Whatever that meant.

I shelved parts of myself. The ones that weren't useful.

I hid them away in a locked room. Deadbolted the door.

Not to keep the world out—but to keep myself in.

I was safer that way.

But I wasn't free.

I still had to navigate him. To stay quiet. Pretend.

I still had to do it all alone.

Until he made the ultimate mistake. Until he embarrassed her. Until he broke the unspoken rules.

Paperwork

In eighth grade, he broke into the old people's church and vandalized it.

The cops came.

My parents had to fix the damage he caused and pay for what he broke.

My mother was pissed.

He had cracked her mask.

That was in the autumn.

In the spring, the state removed him from the house and placed him in a group home.

He wasn't removed because of what he did to me.

He was removed because of a clerical error.

A psychological evaluation had been missing from his file. The evaluation determined he was unadoptable due to his violent tendencies. The evaluation had never made it to my parents before the adoption was finalized.

So, after he vandalized the church, they used it to fight for his removal.

And they won.

The state took him back but let him keep his adopted name.

When Krista and Staci asked about him being removed, I played my part.

I put on the mask of a grieving *sister.*

But I wasn't grieving. I was relieved.

But I also wasn't stupid.

I knew that just because he was gone didn't mean I was safe.

My mother blamed me after he left.

If I displeased her, if I disrespected her, if I defended myself, she smacked me.

She looked for any reason to be mad at me.

And I couldn't look at her.

I begged my dad to let me come live with him. I didn't tell him what happened—just that I needed to get away from her.

He knew how hard it was to live with her.

We did a trial run in July.

By that January, I was living with him full-time.

- -

Teen Me stops talking. She watches me, her eyes burning.

"So? Did you feel it?" Her voice is flat, detached.

She steps closer, her breath slow and measured.

I look down, so she can't see the heartbreak in my eyes.

But she already knows it's there.

She waits.

Her breath stays steady. Mine doesn't.

She leans in—just enough.

Then—

"Yeah. And I'm not even done yet."

3.

Cinnamon Raisin Toast

"Had enough yet?"

Teen Me's voice is heavy.

Burdened by all she's had to carry.

She looks...tired.

Not physically.

Soul tired.

The kind of exhaustion that settles deep in your bones. The kind that builds after years of carrying something no one else can see.

Her arms stay crossed tightly over her chest, but her fingers tap against her biceps—an anxious energy barely contained beneath her skin. Her nails are torn, raw. Red-rimmed wounds circle her cuticles.

Her eyes are sharp, but they don't meet mine. She's staring just past me, her jaw tight, the muscle in her cheek twitching.

I take a slow breath before speaking.

"I'm still here."

No reaction.

"I'm not going anywhere."

She exhales sharply through her nose, shaking her head.

"God, you are so fucking annoying."

The words don't have the bite she intends. They land with more exhaustion than venom.

She shifts her weight, uncrossing her arms, letting them fall limply to her sides. Her fingers curl into fists, then flex, then curl again. Like she's trying to decide if she wants to punch something or if it's even worth the effort.

For a second, she just stands there, rolling her shoulders back, testing how much strength she has left.

Then, finally, she lets out a long, tired breath.

"Can we just get this over with?"

She doesn't wait for an answer. She drops to the ground, her body slumping over, curling in on itself. Knees pulled up, arms wrapped around them. She looks small like this. But her eyes—darting, scanning, searching—tell a different story.

She's bracing.

She doesn't trust this.

Doesn't trust *me*.

She's summoning the strength to continue.

She knows she's going to need it.

I know it, too.

I lower myself to the ground, keeping enough distance to make sure she doesn't feel trapped.

"Okay," I say softly.

Her eyes snap to mine, narrowing. I know she's expecting something. She thinks I will say something patronizing, something condescending.

But I don't give her that.

"Let's start when you packed your bags."

She lets out a bitter laugh, shaking her head like she can't believe this is happening.

Then she exhales, long and slow, closing her eyes for just a second— like she's clearing something away.

When she opens them, they are sharp. Focused.

She's ready.

Hope in a Suitcase

It was supposed to feel like relief.

Leaving her house. Leaving her. The memories. The reminders.

She was pissed.

I had cracked her mask, too.

When Dad and I had our trial run in July, she had to explain why I wasn't with them. She ended up on the church prayer list. Turns out, she liked being the victim more than being perfect.

I was so glad to get away from her. I thought leaving would shed this massive weight off my back.

I thought this was the start of something new. A life where I could be seen. Loved. A life where I could finally be…me.

My dad asked me why I wanted to live with him.

This was my chance to tell him what happened. What she put me through.

It was my chance to get help.

But I was scared.

I thought if I told him, it would overwhelm him. He might not let me live with him if he knew. He might be disappointed in me.

Or ashamed of me.

I told him she was impossible to live with. That I was tired of tip-toeing around her emotions. That she would ignore me for days if I messed up.

He nodded like he understood—because he did.

She made him feel small, insignificant, and then cheated on him. Then she blamed him for her behavior.

He knew her tricks quite well.

When I stayed with Dad, my mother felt like she was losing. Like this was a game, and she was losing to him.

I thought that meant I was the prize.

It didn't.

She just wanted to be better than him. To beat him.

She wanted me to stay. She begged me to. She cried and tried to guilt me.

"Look what you're doing to me. You're crushing me."

Words that might sound like something a caring mother would say. Like she was sad I was leaving. I didn't know for certain. But coming out of the mouth of a viper, they sounded ominous.

The closer we got to the moving date, the angrier she got.

She barely spoke to me. I barely looked at her.

She talked about turning my room into a guest room. Picked out paint colors. Mint green.

She painted the walls. I wasn't leaving for two more weeks. She didn't care.

She covered my furniture with tarps. Moved my bed away from the wall.

I watched her take down my curtains. The ones she made, white with small rainbows on them.

I watched her paint over my lavender walls.

She wanted to hurt me. She wanted me to feel replaced. Unimportant.

Joke's on her. I already knew those feelings well.

She started acting excited about me leaving. She told my stepfather they could finally do what they wanted. No more *kid stuff*.

She started planning a trip for the two of them. Florida.

I thought I was hurting her. I thought she was doing all of this because she was hurt that I was leaving.

Or mad she couldn't control me.

I didn't care either way.

On my last night in her house, my mother found something I wrote.

Among other things, I wrote that I hated her.

I did.

She held it in my face. Told me I was an awful kid for doing this to her. That I wouldn't be happy at my dad's. He wouldn't want to deal with my *bullshit*.

She said he'd get mad about my *dramatic behavior*.

And not to come crying to her when it happened.

Like I ever would.

I packed my bags like someone escaping a burning house.

My hands were shaking, but I moved quickly. Determined. Desperate.

I didn't look back when I walked out the door.

I refused to.

If I looked back, I might hesitate. If I hesitated, I might lose my nerve. If I lost my nerve, I might never leave at all.

As I walked to my dad's truck, I could feel her eyes burning into the back of my head.

I stood up straighter. Walked a little more confidently.

When we pulled out of the driveway, I smiled so she could see it.

Fuck her.

A House That Was Never Home

The first night, I felt grateful and anxious at the same time.

Grateful to be there. Grateful to be anywhere other than my mother's. Grateful to be with my dad. For a chance at something better.

My heart pounded in my chest. I didn't know if it was from excitement or anxiety.

I felt fizzy inside, like Pop Rocks were going off inside me. I wanted to scream and jump up and down.

I didn't.

I made sure to help with the dishes. My stepmother seemed to appreciate it. She played a song on the piano, practicing for church. We all watched TV on the couch.

It was strange.

I thought there would have been some sort of *something* on my first night there. I wasn't expecting a party. Just…something said. Instead, everyone went on with life.

Part of me kind of liked that. It meant I wasn't a disruption. I was doing a good job. I was becoming part of the family.

I had a hard time sleeping. My room was kind of spooky. I didn't like how the tree shadows moved on the walls. They looked like monsters.

But I wasn't afraid.

Because I knew scarier monsters. And mine were real.

It was just so quiet.

There were new noises. The furnace. Creaks in the floor. But there were no dogs barking. No one was driving down the gravel road. None of the normal sounds I was used to.

Everything was different.

But I felt the same.

I thought I would feel better the second I left.

I didn't.

I had to keep myself safe. I had to figure out my own mask. I started planning immediately.

How do I fit into this family? How do I learn their routines? How do I need to show up here?

Will they love me? Will they like me? Will I be too much? Not enough?

I needed to get this right. If I didn't, she would be waiting for me.

I wanted so badly to believe that this place was different. That my dad was different.

But I felt like a guest from the moment I arrived.

His house was small—a double-wide trailer at the top of a long gravel hill. The air smelled different here. Dusty, thick with sawdust and hay. It smelled like a life I didn't belong to.

My bedroom had wood-paneled walls. My bed was so tall I had to jump to get on it. I shared a bathroom with my stepsister. She had her makeup all over the counter. I kept my stuff in a toiletry bag.

It wasn't home.

But at least it wasn't my mother's house.

And that was enough.

Keeping Him, Losing Me

For the next four years, I threw myself into my dad's world.

Horses. Farming. Country music. FFA.

I learned every word to "Ain't Goin' Down ('Til the Sun Comes Up)." I judged livestock and was somehow good at judging sheep. I didn't have a secret skill. I just picked the sheep with the floppiest ears.

I wore cowboy boots and Wrangler jeans, the kind with the big leather patch on the ass.

I went on trail rides. Earned ribbons at riding competitions. I spent every second I could in the barn, helping with the horses.

None of it felt like me. But I did it anyway. I wanted to belong.

I followed my training. I shoved the real me aside. I put on my mask.

And I never took it off.

Because I needed to keep Dad close. I needed to be in his orbit.

He was funny. He was kind. He was good. He made my life feel lighter.

He bought me cherry sours when he was out delivering bread to stores. Told me about the pranks he pulled on other delivery drivers.

He took me to horse shows and auctions. We'd get popcorn and guess how much the horses would sell for.

He brought me with him when he sang church songs at the nursing home. He was a terrible singer. I didn't care.

We watched *Dr. Quinn, Medicine Woman,* and *Walker, Texas Ranger* every Saturday night. We ate Neapolitan ice cream on the couch. He always gave me more of the strawberry. It was my favorite.

His hands were rough, calloused from a life of hard work. So strange for someone so soft.

My dad was my lifeline. He was my bright spot.

And I couldn't afford to lose him.

He Showed Up

In high school, I had FFA.

Turns out you can't really be popular if you're in the Future Farmers of America.

I didn't care. I could disappear into distraction.

I competed in public speaking contests. I gave speeches in front of hundreds of people. I won state. I competed in nationals.

I was an officer. Not just at school—but for my entire area.

I was good. Damn good.

And I was doing it completely alone.

No one at home asked about it. No one came to my competitions. No one listened to me practice.

I got used to stepping off the bus after a competition and seeing the other kids run to their parents.

I walked alone to my car.

I thought I was used to it.

Until the governor's conference.

I was speaking at this big agriculture event. A lot of fancy people were there.

I sat at the head table with the governor. I ate dinner with him and his wife.

There were hundreds of people in the audience.

I gave my speech.

It was about using GPS for farming. Over eight minutes long. I had every word memorized.

People liked it.

Then I rode the bus home.

I walked inside. The house was dark. Everyone was already asleep.

The next morning, I found out something I never expected.

My dad had been in the audience.

He never told me he was coming. He never told me he was there.

My stepmother mentioned it in passing at breakfast. Like it wasn't that big of a deal.

It was.

It was a bigger deal than she could ever have imagined.

He showed up.

For the first time in my life, someone showed up for me—just to see me do something special.

Not for bragging rights. Not because he had to. It wasn't for anyone but me.

And I know I will hold onto that moment for the rest of my life.

Because I can count on one hand the number of times someone showed up for me with no ulterior motive.

Almost every single time—

it was him.

Dreams

I knew I was different.

I had always known.

I was nerdy and loved to read. I wanted to know everything about the world.

I read the dictionary. Almost every *World Book Encyclopedia*. I wanted to learn about life outside my bubble.

Something inside me has always wanted more.

A bigger life. A different life. Something beyond gravel roads and horse barns.

And I think he saw it, too.

When I talked about going to college, he got quiet. When I dreamed out loud about moving away, his face changed.

His eyes got sadder. His energy shifted.

He explained why leaving wasn't realistic. He found ways to bring me back down to his reality.

A reality where college was expensive. Where money was tight.

He said college was for the smart kids. The ones who could solve big equations.

I wasn't good at math. My stepmother often reminded me.

I started to shrink. I began keeping those dreams to myself. I learned that my desire for something different was an insult to my dad.

I learned to see my future through his eyes.

I decided I would stay close. Probably work a job in town—like a bank teller. Or a grocery store cashier.

I would go to their church on Sundays. I would marry a farmer.

It wasn't what I wanted.

But if it was the price for keeping him close—

I believed I could pay it.

The Makeover

When my stepmother first implied I was ugly, I thought she was making a joke.

Then it became a regular thing.

Comments about my weight. Telling me I would be prettier if I fixed my hair more. Constantly judging me for not wearing makeup.

"You're never going to get a boyfriend looking like that!"

What a fucking bitch.

My dad wasn't much help. He didn't criticize me, but he didn't stop her from doing it either.

She hated my clothes. My hair. My face.

And she never let up.

She didn't understand me.

She was always put together. Her salt-and-pepper hair was often up in a bun or a braid. Her makeup always looked fresh.

She sold Mary Kay and tried to get me to use it.

She even gave me a makeover once.

It was actually nice for a bit.

She sat in front of me, spreading the foundation across my face. It felt thick. Like my skin couldn't breathe.

I sat there as she talked about blending and blushes. I didn't really understand.

My mother never taught me about makeup. She never bought me makeup. I never asked her to.

My stepmother started talking about eye shadows. She held onto me to steady herself when she put on eyeliner. Her hand pressed firmly against my collarbone.

A simple touch. A nothing touch.

But my body reacted before my brain caught up.

My chest tightened. My stomach swirled.

A memory flickered—too fast to fully see, but the carpet was purple. A wave of nausea rose in my throat.

My entire body froze.

My muscles stiffened. I tried to swallow, but my throat was dry. I tried to calm myself down, but my mind raced.

I couldn't follow a single thought.

It was like they were all screaming at the same time.

Disorienting.

Like strobe lights flashing in my mind.

Suddenly, my stepmother was back in front of me. I tried to focus on her face, but I couldn't.

It felt like all the air had been sucked out of the room. My chest tightened over my pounding heart.

I clenched my fists, pressing my nails into my palm.

I could push through this. I had to.

But my breath kept coming too fast, my vision started to blur, and I knew—

I was losing.

I asked to go to the bathroom.

I needed to get a hold of myself. My mask was cracking.

I sat on the toilet, pretending to pee.

I started counting.

One, two, three, four, five. Deep breath in.
One, two, three, four, five. Deep breath out.

I kept counting until I calmed down.

I flushed the toilet. Went to the sink and looked in the mirror.

I stared at my face, covered in makeup.

I didn't recognize myself.

I washed my hands. Went back out and sat back in the chair.

She finished the makeover.

I told her I loved it.

Betrayal

I can pinpoint the exact second I lost him.

I don't even remember what we were arguing about at first, but my stepmother and I were in the kitchen, and, like always, she turned the conversation into something about me.

She compared me to my stepsister—a literal beauty queen. She kept going on and on about me not wearing makeup. Not fixing my hair the way she thought I should.

I told her I wasn't interested in all of that. I was more of a tomboy. I told her I was more interested in learning about the world than learning about makeup.

"It's no wonder you're at home on Saturday nights. I mean, look at you."

Her face twisted with genuine disgust.

I finally snapped. I made a sarcastic comment. It was petty.

I implied my stepsister was a slut.

I'm not proud of it. I just wanted my stepmother to shut up.

And then she hit me.

She punched me in the face. Right there, in the kitchen. Right in front of my dad.

And he said nothing.

I grabbed my cheek, shocked. I couldn't believe what had just happened. My mind ran away from me. My face burned.

She stormed off to their bedroom at the back of the trailer, slamming the door.

He kept eating his cinnamon raisin toast like nothing had happened.

I yelled at him. He told me not to curse at him.

I couldn't believe he just sat there without saying a word.

He wasn't surprised. He wasn't even angry.

He was hungry.

Hours later, he sat at the edge of my bed. He asked if I was okay. He looked at my face. A red mark lingered on my cheek.

His eyes looked sad. I thought he finally understood. Maybe he finally got it. Maybe he finally figured out I needed him to protect me.

He sighed.

"I wish you wouldn't have said that. You made things more complicated."

Complicated. For him.

He told me to apologize. To the woman who punched me.

He told me if I didn't apologize, it would make it hard for me to stay. He said I needed to clean up the mess I made.

My heart shattered. His words hurt more than her fist.

He was the person I loved more than anyone. The one who made me feel lighter.

But he didn't protect me or stick up for me.

He blamed me.

He wanted me to apologize. To make his life easier. He wanted it to be my fault.

After he left the room, my mind buzzed. My heart pounded. My muscles tightened.

If I didn't apologize, I would have to move out. I would have to go back to my mother's house.

That night, I cried myself to sleep.

I probably should have apologized.

But I didn't.

The next day, I called my mother. She said she'd talk to my stepfather and let me know. She joked about a "trial run."

I hung up the phone with shaking hands.

I didn't want to go back.

But I knew my mother couldn't hurt me. Not like my dad had.

I knew who she was. And I knew how to survive her.

I told my dad I was leaving.

He couldn't look at me. I couldn't look at him either.

My dad had been my lifeline.

And he let me drown.

The Return

I left within a week.

I moved back into my mother's house.

Not because I wanted to. But because I knew the rules there.

I knew how to keep my armor up, how to keep my expectations low.

At my dad's house, I had started to hope. I took off some of my armor with him.

And that was my mistake.

It broke my dad's heart when I told him I was leaving. He asked me to stay. I told him I couldn't. He teared up.

I had never seen him cry before.

I started to cry, too.

His rough hands wiped the tears from my face.

I told him I was just too hurt to stay.

He said he felt like he was losing me.

He didn't know I was already gone.

When I moved back in with my mother, my room was mint green. My purple carpet was now tan. A part of me felt relieved by the changes. The other part knew it didn't matter.

The color was different, but I still felt sick.

My stepfather built a bigger closet while I was gone. My toys were tucked away in a plastic container. It was as though I never existed.

Everything felt familiar and also different. I felt like a guest there, too. I didn't feel wanted. I felt tolerated.

The panic attacks became more severe.

The muscles in my legs would squeeze. My chest would feel like it was caving in. My toes would curl. My thoughts would race. I hyperventilated. Sometimes I would throw up.

I never told my mother.

Then the depression came.

I stopped caring about FFA. About a bigger life. I didn't care about me.

I wanted to disappear.

So, I did.

- -

Teen Me closes her eyes. She lets out an exhausted sigh.

I take a step closer.

"Don't."

Her voice is sharp, but her eyes remain closed. She's expecting me to try to comfort her.

I know better.

"Teen Me, you had to deal with more than anyone ever should.
And you had to do it alone.
You had to be responsible for your own safety.
You had to hide parts of yourself to be loved.
You endured abuse, neglect, and betrayal.
You had your heart broken over and over."

The tears start falling down my cheeks. I don't bother wiping them away.

"And?"

She finally looks up at me. She's empty. The fire is gone. There's nothing left to burn.

She doesn't move when I step forward. But when I reach for her hand, she pulls away.

"You weren't a bad daughter."

She shrugs. Hangs her head. Starts to pick at her thumbnails.

I try again.

"You didn't fail them. They failed you."

"It doesn't feel that way."

Her voice is quieter now. She wraps her arms around her shins, curling in on herself.

"I know. And it won't for a while."

She's worn down. But her battle within is just beginning.

I want to tell her the myriad of ways she saved me.
That the choices she made then are why I am here today.
I want to tell her she's the toughest person I have ever met.
That her fire makes her powerful.

But I know she's too tired to care.

She stays curled up, staring off into space. Like she's trying to disappear.

"You deserved better."

She flinches. Barely.

But then, her eyes meet mine.

She doesn't cry. She doesn't break. She just holds my gaze.

And then, I see it—
a flicker.
A flash of something.

A small ember.

She exhales deeply.

"Yeah. I know."

4.

Suffocation

I look at Teen Me.

She's still curled into a ball. Her body is here with me.

But her mind isn't.

She's staring off into the distance. Dissociating.

I know what she's doing because I still do it, too.

We sit in silence.

She doesn't move. Doesn't blink. Just stares.

Like she's trying to put a puzzle together in her mind—and if she can just get the pieces to fit, everything will be okay.

Her look is one of desperation. Like she's searching for an exit that doesn't exist. A way out of the labyrinth in her mind. The prison she's built for herself. The one she can't escape.

I break the silence.

"What are you working on up there?"

I point to her head.

She snaps back, blinking hard.

A blank look washes over her face. Like she didn't even realize she was gone.

"What?"

Her voice is flat. Quiet. Like it traveled a long way to get here.

"I was just saying you seemed deep in thought a minute ago. I wondered what you were thinking about."

I watch her carefully. I wonder if she'll share anything with me—or just disappear again.

To my surprise—

she starts talking.

The Disappearing Act

No one ever saw. I made sure of that.

I hid the panic attacks. I made this new/old life work. I was surviving. And that was all I needed to do.

I took every shift I could because it meant I didn't have to be near my mother.

I was nineteen, working as an EMT in the ER, spending every waking moment at the hospital. Sixty-plus-hour work weeks were fine with me.

I liked being in the ER. I liked that it was busy. It meant I would barely be noticed. Easier to disappear that way.

I worked nights. It paid more per hour. And put my mother and me on opposite schedules. Easier to avoid her.

Things had been tense since I had moved back in, but now? Now, my mother was done with me.

I was making real money—not minimum wage, not the kind of job where people could still call me a kid. I was making the kind of money that kept the lights on in houses like hers.

And in her mind, that meant I should be on my own.

She constantly reminded me that I was an adult now. I was making money, so I had no excuse.

I didn't argue. I just disappeared. Into work. Into myself.

I found ways to make sure I was never home. Because every time I was, I still felt like the twelve year old hiding behind a deadbolted door.

I felt trapped in the space where my *brother* had touched me. Sleeping in the same room.

The memories came inconsistently. Some days, I didn't think about it at all. Other days, I couldn't think about anything else.

I felt on edge at my mother's house. Every sound amplified. My muscles were always rigid. I jumped at loud noises.

I didn't understand why.

Am I going crazy? Would that be such a bad thing? I decided it wouldn't be.

At least I would have an excuse for feeling this shitty.

I started having bad dreams. Sometimes I drowned. I would wake up gasping for air. Sometimes I was chased.

I didn't know what was behind me. I just knew to run.

One time, I couldn't. My legs wouldn't move. I looked at my feet, but they wouldn't go.

It was coming. Whatever it was, it wanted me. I could feel it.

It was him.

I never saw his face, but I knew it was him.

I don't know if he caught me. I can't remember. But I woke up shaking.

I peed the bed.

I didn't tell anyone. I just washed the sheets. And shoved the shame down deep.

I was scared. I wanted to say something to someone. I wanted to ask for help. I knew I needed it.

But who was I going to ask?

Who did I feel safe with?

My boyfriend's mom was nice to me. But I would never tell her. She already had enough to deal with.

I didn't really have many friends. Just Michelle and Ashley.

I couldn't tell them.

I didn't want them to know. I didn't want them to think I was messed up or broken. I didn't want them to treat me like I was.

So, I worked extra shifts to avoid going home. I stayed at my boyfriend's house more often. I ate dinner with his family.

They talked to me like I was already their daughter-in-law. The ring on my left hand said I would be soon.

A Life Chosen For Me

When my boyfriend's dad bought a house near my high school, he told me he wanted me to move in and pay rent. It was twenty minutes from my mother's house.

It felt too easy. Like a trick.

But then my mother encouraged it. My stepfather told me to take the deal. He said I owed my boyfriend's dad for doing something nice for me.

Everyone decided for me. I was going to live there. I just had to agree.

So, I did. And I even acted excited about it.

I didn't agree to live there because I wanted to. I agreed because it was easier. To shut my mother up. To get away from her.

But part of me didn't want to live there. A part of me felt like I would be trapped in a life I didn't want. A life that would never feel like it belonged to me.

The house was small. White. A starter home.

It reminded me of a box waiting to be wrapped for the holidays.

Lifeless.

Like me.

Waiting to be sealed shut, so it could pretend to be something it wasn't.

It had a tiny front yard. A rusty carport.

Everything about the house felt small. And when I stepped inside it, so did I.

The air felt thick and stale with emptiness.

It felt like walking into someone else's life, putting on their clothes, and trying to make them fit. I knew they didn't. But I didn't know what other option I had.

No one taught me how to live on my own. At least this way, I had my boyfriend's parents to help me learn the things I'd need to know.

I felt like an ungrateful piece of shit.

I had a place to stay. A house they bought with me in mind. I felt grateful to get away from my mother. Grateful someone would do something like that for me.

But I never packed my things to move. Every time I tried, it felt like I was dying inside. Like this house might take what little I had left.

I wasn't excited. Or hopeful.

I didn't think, *This is a new beginning.*

I just thought, *This is what I'm supposed to do. This is what comes next.*

Like a playlist of songs. Automatically moving to the next track.

This was going to be a song on my playlist. I didn't have to like the song. I just had to let it play.

Because skipping wasn't an option.

Adulting

It never really felt like it was possible to live on my own before.

Sure, I could have gotten an apartment. I could have afforded rent.

But I didn't.

I was afraid.

I didn't know if I could handle carrying all the things that happened to me *plus* figuring out how to be an adult. It seemed like too much at once.

I had barely paid a bill at this point. I had never had a credit card. I had bounced checks because I didn't understand how withdrawals worked.

I didn't understand some of the most basic things I thought adults were supposed to know.

And on top of all of that?

I was still afraid of making my mother mad.

I had to leave the right way. In a way that kept her mask safe. In a way that kept *my* mask safe.

Because if I did it wrong—she would make me regret it.

From the outside looking in, it all made sense. My chances of failing were low. My boyfriend's family would be my support system.

Staying at the rental house meant I wouldn't have to pay a security deposit. I wouldn't have to pay first and last month's rent upfront. I would have a landlord who gave me the benefit of the doubt.

I just had to pack my stuff and go. But I couldn't do it.

My mother told me I'd be stupid not to take such a deal.

She gave me a deadline.

I had until summer.

She didn't care where I went.

She just wanted me gone.

The House That Wasn't Mine

I remember the first time I went to the rental house alone. I let myself in. I had a key.

It was in the final stages of renovation. Still some minor touch-up painting to do.

I stood in the living room on the new shaggy carpet—tan with little specks of blue and brown. It was soft under my feet.

I had been buying furniture from classified ads and Craigslist. Someone else's furniture felt appropriate for what felt like someone else's life. I tried to envision where I'd put everything. The couch against the wall, the chair by the front window.

The pieces seemed to fit. Why didn't I?

I stared at the walls. At the stacked washer and dryer near the fridge.

It never felt like mine. It never felt like a home I was meant to live in.

But I didn't think that was a problem.

I was used to living in places that didn't feel like I belonged.

I wondered about the people who lived in the house before me.

Had they felt trapped in their lives, too?
Had they thought about dying, too?
Did they wish it would all stop?

Those thoughts were coming up more often.

Standing in line at the grocery store, I'd see people I knew. Of course, I did. That's how small towns work.

I would look at them and wonder:

Would they go to my funeral?
Would my dad cry?
Would my mother?
What would my sister tell my nephew?

I felt like I was disappearing right in front of everyone, and no one ever noticed.

I desperately wanted to be seen.

But I was also proud that I couldn't be.

It meant my mask was working. My training was working.

Even as I stood there, I felt like a guest in my own life.

I could see how it all played out: I would keep working as an EMT. Eventually become a flight medic. I would marry my high school boyfriend. We would live in this house. Start a life together.

I mean, there are dozens of movies about the woman who runs off for a big life only to come back where it all began. Only to find real happiness in what she ran from.

Reese Witherspoon had just made one. Her story took place in Alabama, though.

Wasn't I supposed to want this?

The classic American story? Marry my high school sweetheart and settle down?

And as that thought settled in, I felt like I was being swallowed whole.

Like whatever remaining parts of me I had been holding onto were slipping away.

Like I was losing myself.

And the worst part?

I didn't even care.

I just needed out. I just needed to be away from my mother. Away from the memories. Away from the fact that no matter how much time had passed, I still felt dirty when I was there.

It had been years since my *brother* hurt me. But every minute I spent in my mother's house made it feel like it had never stopped.

I stood in the starter home, my toes curling onto the new carpet. The room smelled like fresh paint.

It felt like the start of a new song. One I already knew the words to.

I looked around. Walked into each of the rooms.

Two bedrooms. One bathroom. A kitchen. A living room.

I tried to see my life here.

Would I spill pancake batter on the counters?

Would I put my Christmas tree in this corner? Or that one?

Would I dance in my pajamas in the living room?

I tried to convince myself this was just another house. Just another room. Just another start.

Could I feel alive here?

I already knew the answer. Or at least my body did.

My breath went shallow. Then distant. I forgot to breathe. Just for a second. My body was back underwater.

Thrashing.

Searching for the surface.

My heart raced. My hands shook.

I snapped back.

I looked at the living room walls.

White. Sterile. Colorless.

I saw my life here. It was already planned. I just had to accept it.

Or I had to find another way out.

Turns out, I can drown on dry land.

Deep Thoughts

You know that *SNL* skit with Stuart Smalley? The one where he goes, "I'm good enough. I'm smart enough. And doggone it, people like me."

I always wondered what it would be like to have a voice like that in your head.

Mine was much meaner. Cruel, even. Like my mother.

Those thoughts started to stick around.

Like static in my brain. Like white noise I couldn't turn off.

Actually, it was more like *dark* noise.

The first time, it felt intrusive. Quick. Fleeting. Gone before I could grasp it.

But then it came back.

Again and again.

I wondered if my brain was trying to tell me something. Like—*was this the plan all along?* Maybe I wasn't supposed to live a long life.

I started playing out the scenarios.

Not planning, exactly. Just…wondering.

If I wrecked my car, would it look like an accident? How fast would I have to go? Would anyone be able to tell?

What if I took too many pills and just went to sleep? Would that be easier to handle? No mess.

Would it feel like a gift? No one would have to deal with my bullshit anymore.

I'd stop being so annoying. I'd stop being a brat. They'd probably like that.

Would my dad cry? Would my mother? Would anyone?

What would my sister tell my nephew?

Would people at work be shocked? Would they say I seemed fine? Would they say they never saw it coming?

I thought about it all the time.

I stopped feeling afraid of the thoughts. They started to feel like relief.

And then one day, a girl came into the ER.

One who swallowed the bottle of Tylenol. She didn't mean to die.

Not really.

I think she just wanted to stop hurting.

I understood that kind of desperation.

I watched her mother break in front of me. In front of the entire ER.

She fell to the floor. Screaming. Wailing.

I saw the grief crack her open from the inside.

And I thought—

If I did it, would my mother break? Would she wail like that? Would she even care?

I couldn't imagine my mother crying like that. Not for me.

But I knew she'd do it for attention.

Maybe that should've hurt.

But it didn't.

After seeing that mother cry, something inside me shifted.

It wasn't some monumental shift.

The thoughts didn't go away. Not at first.

They were just as loud. Forceful. Frequent.

But it was enough of a shift for me to pause.

It was enough for me to hold on.

The Offer

I knew I had to get away. But I couldn't live in that rental house.

I knew I would never breathe properly if I lived there. Like the air couldn't fully inflate my lungs there.

I had to get away from my mother's house. Out of that town.

I had to get out of this version of my life before it swallowed me whole. Or put in a grave.

And then, one night—

I met him.

I was working a shift in the ER. He was a medical student. On his last rotation. Leaving in six weeks.

He asked me to go, too.

And without even thinking—

I said yes.

- -

Teen Me got silent again.

The blank look returned to her face.

She had returned to her puzzle, looking for the right piece to make her feel whole.

I knew she wouldn't find it. But she didn't.

It would be another version of me that made that realization.

"Teen Me?"

Her expressionless face turned. Her eyes met mine.

I could see the exhaustion. The fear. The need to prove her worth. The desperate need to be seen. To feel like she existed somewhere outside of her mind.

But I could also see her strength.
Her bravery.
Her fire.
Her relentless spirit.
Her trust that she'd get through it all.

Because she had to.

I was sitting right in front of her, seeing her fully for the first time.

I could see her complexity. I could finally see her with compassion. But I wondered if she'd ever be able to see the same.

Would she ever see her own magic?

She exhaled, long and slow.

"Is that it?"

Her voice was flat, but I caught the tension beneath it.

She was holding it all inside: The exhaustion. The anger. The unbearable weight of everything she carried alone.

I waited before answering.

She wasn't asking if our conversation was over.

She was asking if this was it. If this was what all the pain, all the fighting, all the pushing through had led to.

This?

I didn't have an answer she'd want to hear. But the silence gave her the answer anyway.

"I don't know. But I'd like to think so."

She let out a short, sharp laugh. Not the kind born of amusement, but the kind meant to cut.

"Yeah. That's what I thought."

Her eyes flickered, searching my face for something. A reason to trust me. A reason to believe it wasn't all for nothing.

I wished I could give her proof.

She stared at me for another moment before looking away, her jaw tightening, her fingers twitching.

I didn't push her.

I knew she wasn't done with me.

She wasn't done being angry.

But for now—

she was tired.

And so, she let it be.

5.

Breathe

I see her already.

She looks ragged.

This isn't like before.

With Little Me, with Teen Me—I could stand apart from them, listen from a distance.

But with her? With 20s Me?

I feel her in my bones.

I don't know what that means yet, but I know it's different.

I approach carefully.

She doesn't even notice I'm there.

Her eyes are distant.

She's lost in a sea of thoughts. Each one worse than the one before.

"20s Me?"

She doesn't respond.

She just sits.

Staring.

"20s Me?" I speak a little louder.

Still nothing.

She's right in front of me, but she's not here.

She's somewhere else.

Somewhen else.

The past? The future?

I can't tell.

But I know she's lost inside it.

I wave my hand in front of her face.

She snaps back.

Confused.

Like she doesn't know how long she's been gone.

Like she doesn't know how she got back.

"20s Me? You okay?"

She looks at me.

Her eyes still have a glaze on them.

It's almost imperceptible.

It probably is to those who don't know her.

"I'm fine," she says.

Her eyes shift for a second.

Like she's trying to recognize her own voice.

She looks at her feet.

It's been a while since I've seen her.

Not as long as Teen Me, but a bit.

She has the same kind of exhaustion as Teen Me. Thick and heavy. A deep, soul-tired.

But hers is different.

It's aged.

Like an old wine with a dry cork.

Still holding everything inside.

It would crumble if someone tried to open it.

"20s Me, I was hoping you could tell me about him."

Her eyes snap to mine.

Her teeth press into her lip.

A tiny, silent act of self-control.

Like if she lets herself speak, the words might come out too fast.

Too messy. Too much.

Her legs start bouncing.

Like there's a concentration of electricity in them.

Like she's running in place.

She starts scratching her thumbnails.

They're just as torn up as Teen Me's.

Bloodied, like she's been trying to climb out of a hole.

But it's only in her mind.

I glance at my own hands.

They're scarred.

My thumbnails are still rough from the scratching.

Some habits aren't worth breaking.

"Why would you want to know about him? You already know. Why would you make me relive that again?" Her voice shakes.

It's a fair question.

"I don't want you to relive it for nothing, 20s Me. I know the story from the memories I carry, but you felt it in your bones. You know what it smelled like. What it sounded like. I want to hear it in your words. I want to listen to your story."

"Why? Is this some sort of therapy project or something?"

Her voice isn't shaking anymore.

It's monotone.

I can't tell if she's being sarcastic.

"It's not a therapy project. It's a *me* project."

She raises an eyebrow.

Like she's trying to understand the difference.

"My therapist didn't ask me to do this. I'm doing it on my own. I'm here because I want to be. Not because I have to be."

Her expression remains unchanged.

Her gaze is still locked on me.

Scanning for the catch.

The bullshit.

I continue: "Here's the thing. My story—our story—is often hard for me to access without wanting to run away. It's hard for me to sit with. It's a fucked-up story. I figured it was probably hard for you to sit with too. I thought maybe we could sit with it together."

She doesn't respond.

She just watches me.

Waiting.

Still scanning.

Still looking for the trap.

"How do we do that? Sit together with it? Are we just quiet together? Do I have to talk? What are you expecting of me here?"

I smile. Just a tiny one.

I know that feeling.

That need to find the "right answer."

The "right way."

"There are no expectations. You share what you want. You can share a lot or a little. Whatever you choose, I'll be here with you. I'll sit with you."

"What if it's too hard to tell?"

Another fair question.

"Then don't tell it. Only tell the parts you feel safe sharing. You can keep the others if you want."

She sits in silence for a long time.

I don't rush her.

"If I say it out loud, does that mean it will go away? That I won't feel like this anymore?"

I know she's a grown woman, but in this moment, she feels like a child.

I won't lie to her.

"No, it won't go away. It may not feel any different to say it out loud. It also might. We won't know until you share your story."

She sighs.

She's never been afraid to jump. But she's always been terrified of falling.

She just needed the right conditions.

The right reason to make the hard choice.

The right reason to take the leap.

The chance that it *could* feel different—must have been the right reason.

She exhales slowly.

Like she's exhaling something more than air.

Like she's weighing the risk.

If saying it out loud will make it real.

If making it real will make it worse.

She glances at me one more time.

One last scan.

Then she begins.

Him

He was funny. Charming. In a nerdy, sci-fi way.

He liked *Star Trek*, just like my stepfather. In so many ways, he felt familiar. But also different.

He grew up in a small town. Bigger than mine, but he understood that world. He didn't grow up worrying about money like I did. He didn't have to walk on eggshells with his parents. He loved them both, and they loved him.

He was driven. He wanted something different. Something bigger.

I knew that feeling. I felt lighter, less guilty, knowing he felt it, too.

When we met, he was scheduled to work in the ER for the month. The last month before he was going to graduate. We started talking on his first night there.

We would sit in the doctor's area in the middle of the night and talk. I felt special sitting in there with him. Like I was somewhere I shouldn't have been, but because I was with him, it was okay.

I was a nobody who got to be a somebody with him.

He was easy to talk to, and he seemed interested in what I had to say. He talked about adult things with me: Retirement. Politics. The world.

He was well-read. He could sing. He wasn't afraid to be silly.

He was proud to introduce me to his friends. A couple of weeks into dating, he took me to a party to meet them. I got drunk and fell down some concrete steps. I hit my head. Got a concussion.

He took me to the ER—not the one I worked at, because he didn't want my coworkers to see me.

I thought that was nice of him. He was protecting me, and he barely knew me.

He stayed with me at the hospital. He made sure to wake me up every few hours.

Later, he made me a mixed CD of songs. Like he wanted to impress me.

He was from a world close enough to mine to feel safe, but far enough away to feel big. I wanted to learn everything he knew. Understand the world the same way he did.

He felt sophisticated.

And he wanted me.

He Came Back

We had a great conversation during a night shift in the ER.

We talked about travel. About seeing the world.

I told him I had always wanted to go to Iceland. I didn't even have to tell him the capital city. He already knew.

He told me the Galápagos Islands were his dream trip. I filed that away. I had research to do.

We talked about why he wanted to become a doctor. What it was like to go to medical school. What college was like for him.

I listened to memorize every word. Searing his stories into my brain to interrupt my dark thoughts. The ones I would never tell him about.

When the shift was over, we went our separate ways.

Then he came back.

Caught me before I left.

Asked me to have breakfast at a nearby diner.

I said yes. I didn't even have to think about it.

He had already done something special. Something I never expected.

He came back for me.

The Diner

At the diner, I ordered pancakes but barely ate any. The butterflies in my stomach beat their wings too hard.

But they didn't quite drown out the pangs of guilt.

I had a boyfriend. And I was sitting with another man, feeling more alive than I had in months.

I knew I shouldn't be in that diner. But I wanted to stay. To never leave. To keep close to him. To remain in his orbit.

Things felt quieter there, with him. Strange, considering the morning rush.

Plates clattered. People talked. Servers called out orders to the kitchen. Cheap coffee brewed.

I felt a million miles away from the sounds of gravel and the smell of freshly tilled soil.

I couldn't take it all in. I wanted to be present with him. Listen to every word. Feel light and breezy. The way he was making me feel.

I kept telling myself, *It's just breakfast. He's just a coworker like any other.*

But the guilt was eating at me.

I wasn't cheating, right? Or was I?

If I wasn't, then why did I feel so ashamed to be there? So unworthy?

I knew I shouldn't be there with him. It would hurt my boyfriend. I wasn't the person who did these kinds of things.

But he felt clean. Untouched by the darkness within me.

Could I feel that way if I stayed near him? Could I finally feel clean?

I wasn't sure, but I needed to find out.

So, I stayed in the diner with him. Laughing. Sharing my stories. Only the good ones.

I wasn't the girl who was dying inside when I was with him. The girl who came from the fucked-up family. The fuckup.

After breakfast, we said goodbye. I went home.

I smiled the entire drive back to my mother's house. I finally knew what it felt like to breathe fresh air.

That's what he was like. The first breath of air after opening the windows in a stale house.

I almost drove straight to my boyfriend's house to break up with him right then.

I stopped myself.

I worried I was being impulsive. I decided to see how I felt after getting some sleep.

When I woke up, the butterflies lingered. My smile remained. I couldn't keep it hidden.

If he could make me smile while sitting in the very room I used to deadbolt, that was enough for me.

That felt like salvation. He felt like salvation.

I broke up with my boyfriend later that day. I broke his heart. I told his dad I wouldn't be moving into the rental house. And I didn't think twice about any of it.

Pieces

Nothing felt strange about him.

If anything, he felt like a piece I had been looking for. Not *the* piece, but *a* piece.

I felt closer to being whole with him. Closer to someone I wanted to be.

The difference between him and my boyfriend was stark. My boyfriend felt like a concrete block. Like the ones they tie to people's feet in mobster movies. Dragging a body to the bottom of the ocean. Food for the fishes.

It wasn't my boyfriend's fault. He was a nice guy. A good guy. He would be good for someone else.

Just not me.

I told myself I was doing him a favor by breaking up with him. He wouldn't have to deal with my crazy anymore. My panic attacks. My mother. He could finally be free of me and all of my baggage.

But this new thing felt different.

After the diner, after the parties, after meeting his friends—this guy who was about to be a doctor still wanted me. He still thought I was *something.* That I was *special.*

He felt *lighter.* He felt like the *lifeline* I had been looking for. He felt like the one who would keep me from drowning.

He would hold my hand while he drove. His palms would sweat. Like he was nervous. I found it endearing.

Sometimes I would look at his hands. They looked so different from my dad's.

They weren't calloused from a life of hard work. They were smooth from a life of privilege.

I would look at his hands and wonder—

Are these the hands that will pull me out of the depths? The ones to hold me close? The ones to shield me?

I hoped so.

I didn't need him to protect me forever. Just long enough for me to take some armor off and *breathe.*

Starting Over

We moved to another state six weeks after meeting.

I barely had time to meet his parents. He barely had time to meet mine.

He didn't like my mother. He thought she might have Borderline Personality Disorder. He told me as we were driving away from her house.

It awed me that he could diagnose people with such ease. He knew so much about so much.

I wondered how he would diagnose *me.*

I'd better keep the mask tight

I didn't want to give him a reason to leave.

We moved into an apartment near the riverfront. My first time living in a city.

In the evenings, I would feed the ducks. I named the white ones Preston. I don't know why. But he liked it. He started calling them Preston too.

A couple of weeks after we moved, he started his residency. Internal Medicine. I went to fancy dinners with other residents and faculty. He worked long hours.

I was alone a lot.

I didn't like being with my thoughts while he was gone. That's when the dark noise roared. When the scary thoughts would come back. The ones where I pictured my funeral. But now he was always in the front row.

I didn't tell him about my struggles. I didn't tell him what I went through. Why would I? I didn't want that world anywhere near this one.

We got a puppy to keep me company. A brown dachshund named Bailey. We bought him from my mother. Saving him from a life in her puppy mill.

Growing up, I didn't realize she had a puppy mill. I just knew there were always puppies around, and I liked them.

Besides, everyone had a lot of animals. Krista's family had pigs. My mother had puppies. Then I learned what a puppy mill was. That many of the dogs never got to put their feet on the ground. Their paws mangled and deformed by a life on wire.

I remembered her dog runs. Wire cages suspended above the ground. Easier to clean with a hose. Plywood boxes to keep them warm in the winter.

I felt sick to my stomach.

How could I have grown up on a fucking puppy mill and not realized something was off? How did I not *see* it?

Once, I brought up how disgusting and harmful puppy mills were. How they were cruel and inhumane.

She slapped me across the face.

And reminded me that's how she bought the Guess jeans I was wearing.

So when we decided to get a puppy, we bought it from her. Getting the puppy anywhere else would have infuriated her.

I had to protect her emotions. I had to follow the rules. Even when I lived six hours away.

I specifically wanted a puppy she couldn't sell. I knew those were the ones she kept for breeding stock.

Bailey was tiny. Likely the runt of his litter. He also had a crooked tip on his tail. Just enough to make him *not good enough.*

I understood that feeling.

We picked up Bailey on New Year's Day. A quick trip, in and out. We had to get back. He had a call week coming up in the hospital.

He got jealous of Bailey. He told me when he was home, he wanted my attention.

I made sure he had it. Snuggles with Bailey would have to wait.

I had plenty of time when he was working. I was still trying to figure out what I would do for work.

I needed to take a test to be an EMT in our new state. He encouraged me to switch careers. He didn't like the idea of me in high-stress situations.

I didn't argue. Fine by me. At least, that's what I told myself.

I didn't have qualifications for much. I got a job at a sports bar on the riverfront. Not far from home. Not far from Bailey.

I worked as a server and a bartender. It wasn't how I imagined my life.

But it was *enough*.

- -

20s Me quiets.

She's processing. I'm not sure what. I consider asking, but I stop myself.

She looks at me. Really looks at me. Her eyes, tired. The glaze remains there, like a film between her and the world. Like she's seeing me, but not really seeing me.

She exhales slowly.

"Can we take a break?" Her voice is softer than before. Less defensive. *"I need a minute."*

I smile gently. "Of course. Take all the time you need."

She gives me the smallest nod, then looks away.

I watch as she slips into the darkness. I know she'll stay there until I call for her again. She knows how to navigate that space.

She doesn't mind it.

It's all she's ever known.

6.

The Click

I wait as 20s Me slips back into the darkness—the only place she ever felt safe.

She lingers there, hovering at the edges of my awareness. Not gone. But not fully present. Somewhere in between.

I feel her hesitation. Like she's deciding whether stepping forward again is worth it.

The dark tugs at her like a familiar blanket. She's spent years wrapping herself in it.

I wonder if she's already had enough of this. Enough of being in the light. Enough of being seen.

The light often feels scarier than the dark.

So, I let her be.

I sit there, planning a yoga class in my mind, waiting for her return.

A sequence. A breath pattern. A theme.

Anything to keep me from calling for her too soon. Anything to keep me from rushing her.

And then—

"I think I'm ready to continue."

Her quiet voice quivers.

I wait for her to step into the light.

She doesn't.

She wants to stay in the dark while she shares what comes next.

I understand why.

"You have my full attention," I tell her.

I rub my fingertips together, feeling for the ridges of my fingerprints. A strategy to stay anchored in the moment.

This moment.

Because it belongs to her.

She whispers something to herself.

Soft. Steady. A barely-there breath.

"I am capable. I am confident. I am brave."

Affirmations.

She uses them to feel stronger. I know because I use them, too.

A slow, heavy sigh.

Then she continues.

Warnings

I can think of two red flags.

Two times he made me feel like he owned me. Two times I felt grateful that he did.

The first time, I was working at the sports bar.

Pete Rose came into my section once. He let me sit with him while he bet on football games. He asked me to pick a team.

I don't know why, but I said the Miami Dolphins. They won that day. He gave me a great tip.

A couple of Sundays later, I was working a double shift. The first shift as a server. The second as a bartender.

Some Canadian guys came in. They were in town for an NFL game, celebrating Canadian Thanksgiving. They took a trip together every year, and this year, they ended up here. In my new city. In my section.

They were nice. They talked to me and flirted with me. It was all part of the job.

But he came in to see me. He sat in my section like always. He saw them flirting, and he didn't like it.

I thought it was sweet that he was jealous. I thought it meant I was important to him. That I mattered.

The Canadians paid their bill and headed to the football game. He finished his lunch. He told me he was heading home to sleep. He had worked the night before. He was still in his scrubs.

The Canadians came back after the game. By then, I was behind the bar. They were already drunk and wanted to keep the party going. So they kept ordering drinks. And I kept serving them.

They flirted most of the night. Then, when they were drunk enough, they walked back to their hotel.

I walked out of the bar after my shift and got in my car. I didn't see him in the parking lot at first.

But then I did.

A familiar car. Our home state license plate.

He was there. Tucked away in a corner of the lot.

My stomach dropped.

Why is he here? Am I in trouble? Did I do something wrong?

When I saw him, I walked over. Tapped on the glass. Demanded to know why he was there.

He hung his head in shame and told me he never left. He started to cry. He was worried I was going to leave with the Canadians. That I was going to cheat on him.

My stomach twisted. I had never seen him like this.

The shame. The desperation. The clinging.

It should have made me uneasy. Instead, it made my heart jump.

I mean something to him.

I didn't see it as a red flag. If anything, the flag became greener.

The second time was different.

It felt wrong. I excused it away. But I didn't feel good about it.

We went to a Halloween party together.

All the first-year residents were going. He wanted to make a good impression. He wanted to look like the cool guy.

He wore my grandfather's old smoking jacket. The one I kept after my grandma died. Silk pajama pants. Slippers.

He was going as Hugh Hefner.

I wore fishnet stockings. A strapless spandex bodysuit. My ass cheeks barely peeked out. A headband with bunny ears. A furry tail.

And a trench coat. Because I felt uncomfortable.

I tied the trench coat tightly. Planning to be *cold* the entire night. I didn't want to disappoint him. I didn't want him to think I was a prude. I wanted to seem more secure in my body. To give off the confidence of someone who felt sexy.

The time came. We got inside the party.

He wanted me to take my coat off.

I didn't want to.

He got annoyed. Said that was the whole point of the outfit. Encouraged me to have a couple of drinks. To lighten up.

So I did.

The first drink, my trench coat stayed on.

The second drink, my trench coat came untied.

The third drink, it came off.

"Let's get a few more drinks in her. Let's see what else comes off."

He was joking. At least, I hoped so.

He wanted his friends to stare at me. To want me. To be jealous of what he had.

He told me all of that in the car on the way home.

I was surprised. Proud.

I was something that could make people jealous.

It should have screamed *red flag*. Or at least whispered it.

Instead, my heart skipped a beat.

I should have run.

But I didn't.

Because for the first time in my life, someone *wanted* me.

And I mistook that for love.

Surf & Turf

We got married.

His hometown. His church. His preacher. His friends.

Not many people on my side of the church.

I didn't invite my friends. Not Michelle or Ashley. Not Krista or Staci. I didn't want that life touching this one.

They had to move half of his friends to my side of the aisle. He didn't want me to feel bad about myself. I didn't.

My stepfather walked me down the aisle.

My dad sat on one of the pews. We still weren't speaking. My sister invited him. He surprised me by showing up. It really meant something.

We promised to reconnect when things settled down.

We both knew we wouldn't.

My husband and I went to New York City for our honeymoon. I thought it was fun to call him that. *Husband.*

We stayed at the Waldorf Astoria. I felt like Bette Midler's character in *Big Business*—the small-town twin in awe and wonder, walking through the city like a kid in a fairy tale.

I marveled at the lights. At the buildings. The people.

I marveled at what my life had become.

I went to Broadway musicals and stayed in fancy hotels. I was married to a doctor. I felt different. Like I could stand a little taller. I walked down Fifth Avenue, my stride a little longer.

We went to a really fancy dinner. A steakhouse he read about. They brought the steak out on a trolley. Displayed the cuts of beef. Explained what made each one special.

And then they offered something from the sea.

He made a joke about what happens when a woman orders surf and turf. The server didn't laugh. I only half-smiled.

The server held up a lobster that had been sitting on a lettuce leaf. When they picked it up, its legs squirmed. It had been alive the whole time. Silently suffering. For God only knows how long.

We ordered our steaks. They wheeled the trolley away. Spritzing the lobster with water as they walked. Elongating its suffering. Preparing it for the next table of hungry eyes.

I couldn't shake the image of the lobster.

Why would they do that? We all know what a lobster looks like. Why would you suffocate it just so we could see what we already knew?

I felt nauseous. Guilty.

I told him it made me uncomfortable to see a living creature squirm like that. It actually hurt me to see it.

He got annoyed. Told me he was excited for this dinner and I better not ruin it.

I didn't bring it up again.

But it was too late.

The energy shifted. His tone of voice changed. He became more assertive. Angrier.

I needed to get in line.

Not because he said it. I just knew it.

I knew I needed to eat my steak. I needed to act normal.

So, I did.

Smart

I messed up a lot.

I was naïve about the world. I didn't understand how a lot of things worked.

I said *seen* instead of *saw*—a lot. He corrected me every time. He blamed my *hillbilly upbringing.*

Sometimes, he found it endearing. He would giggle like we had an inside joke. His face would soften. His voice would turn kinder, like he was talking to a child.

Sometimes, it frustrated him. Those were the times I locked the bedroom door. Hid in the closet on the floor. Two doors between him and me.

The closet didn't make me feel safe.

I never felt safe when he got like that.

But sitting in the closet made him quieter. Put more distance between me and the names he was calling me.

Stupid.

A waste of his fucking time.

Bitch.

Trash.

Stupid was his favorite. He called me that all the time.

He loved to point out the things I didn't know. The gaps in my knowledge. The times I wasn't informed about what was going on in the world.

"My God. Do I have to teach you everything?"

"It's not that hard to understand."

"C'mon, you're not really that dumb, are you?"

He did it in front of others. Always milder. But always there.

"You'll have to forgive my wife. She's not a fan of reading."

"Good thing she's cute."

I began obsessively reading the news. *The New York Times. The Washington Post. The Atlantic.* CNN.

I wanted to know everything happening in the world. I didn't want to be *stupid.* An embarrassment. A thing he had to explain to others.

I started college at a local university. No more working at the sports bar. No more flirty customers. Just school. I was going to be a teacher.

My father-in-law told me I'd be a good one. I didn't know what I wanted to do. So I figured I might as well get my summers off.

I was doing well in college. Straight As. But I still wasn't smart enough.

I still messed up. I was still stupid.

He said it all the time. Insinuated it daily.

Stupid became a fog over everything. Barely visible. But I felt it. The cold, gray air. Painful in my lungs.

It washed over me every single time he said it.

Stupid.

Stupid.

Stupid.

All I wanted to know was what it took to be *smart.*

Wendy's

I did my fair share of arguing. I tried to hold my ground with him. Tried to show him I could spar at his level. That I could match him intellectually.

I never could. He always found a way to win.

We were driving to his parents' house by the lake. He was behind the wheel, like always. He got carsick if he wasn't driving. I liked it when he drove. Less responsibility.

We stopped at Wendy's. I needed to pee.

"We'll go in, use the bathroom, and grab the food to go," he said.

He parked in the lot, then asked what I wanted to eat.

"I'll take a taco salad," I told him.

He started laughing like I was joking. I didn't get the joke. I was serious.

A glint flashed in his eye. Like a cat about to pounce.

"Who the fuck orders a taco salad to eat in the car?"

I just looked at him.

"What kind of idiot orders a taco salad for the car?" His voice got louder.

"In what world would it make sense to eat a taco salad on a road trip?"

I pointed out that it was on the drive-through menu. "The first word is drive," I said, thinking I was being clever.

He disagreed.

I felt his hand cross my face. Hot and fast.

I gasped. Stunned.

I might not have even believed it was real—except that I heard it. Loud and clear.

A sound that anchored itself into my bones. A sound that still echoes when I go to sleep. A sound that immediately told me—

I had left one cage and walked into another.

There was no denying it. No justifying it.

He had just hit me. Over a taco salad.

I didn't cry right away.

I sat there, ears ringing, my face burning, my brain scrambling.

It didn't make sense. None of it made sense.

But the longer the silence stretched, the more it did.

He hit me, and the world didn't stop. The world didn't even flinch.

I stared at my lap. Waited for the car to start moving again. Waited for the moment to correct itself.

It didn't.

I was still breathing. The world was still spinning. Somewhere, someone was laughing.

This was just a moment.

Are other people having moments like this too? Are they happening right now?

I felt something building inside me. Like a balloon stretched too tight.

Like a scream trapped inside a throat.

I finally started to cry.

Bent forward in the passenger seat. Tried to curl into myself.

My mind raced, trying to understand what had just happened. Trying to understand what I had done wrong.

He didn't say anything. Just sat there in silence.

The engine hummed. My breath hiccupped in my chest.

My face burned where he hit me, but my body refused to move.

He sat right there next to me. In the driver's seat. Close enough to touch.

But it felt like he was a thousand miles away.

Still, nothing.

He just stared ahead. As if I hadn't just learned something about him I could never unlearn.

I cried.

And cried.

And cried.

I kept trying to make the tears stop. But they fell anyway.

I looked at my feet. Shifted in my seat. Started picking at my thumbnails.

"I'm sorry."

His voice broke the silence. It surprised me.

"I shouldn't have done that. I'm ashamed."

He started to cry. It wasn't anything new. He was always emotional.

He begged me to forgive him. Told me it would never happen again. He loved me. He'd be lost without me.

I told him it was okay. I told him I forgave him.

But I knew it was wrong. I knew it was a bad sign.

I comforted him to ease his guilt. Rubbed his back while he cried.

I told him I was okay. Told him it wasn't that big of a deal.

Told myself the same thing.

I didn't get a taco salad.

But I did leave a piece of my dignity in a Wendy's parking lot somewhere in Indiana.

Bailey

He always said he would never do it again.

He would always cry. He would always tell me how he was stressed. Or exhausted. Or that the anger just got to be too much. Or that it was because he had been drinking.

He would say he was getting it under control.

Then he would blame it on me. He would say if I didn't make him ask for things all the time, life would be easier. That these were things a smart person would have known. But I was stupid.

I must have been. Because I could never find the right balance to make him happy. Some things would work sometimes, but not always. Other times, those same things would get me in trouble.

His temper was an invisible line that kept moving. Not only was I never going to cross it, but I was never going to catch it either.

He would buy me things. That was his love language: stuff.

The bruise on my wrist from where he twisted my arm? That got me a pair of shoes.

The mark on the wall where he pushed me? A new purse.

That was how it went: I would mess up. He would react. He would apologize. He would buy me something. He would be calm again. I would mess up. And the cycle would continue.

Sometimes, the good days lasted longer than the bad. Sometimes, they didn't. Back-to-back bad days. Or weeks.

Thank God for Bailey. His sweet puppy face had aged. White hairs mixed with his brown fur. He grew older.

Had I?

Time blurred together. It always did.

Bailey loved me. And he didn't like him.

Bailey never trusted him. Like he could see what I couldn't. Or wouldn't.

Bailey would drag trash from the kitchen into his closet. And poop in his shoe. One time, he even pooped in his lap.

That one was a problem.

I had to scoop Bailey up and hide in the closet for a while after that.

He was furious. Yelling. Banging.

I put my trust in a construction-grade door. I needed it to hold.

He threatened to take Bailey away. To make me give him up.

I sat on the floor of the closet holding Bailey. Both of us shook.

I hugged him close. Whispered that it was going to be okay. Promised we would always be together.

I told Bailey I would die before giving him up.

Will it come to that?

I honestly didn't know.

Two Worlds

He left me places so many times I lost count.

At a bar. On a street.

If he got angry about traffic, I would start thinking about how to get home. How to get back to Bailey after he left me somewhere.

It felt inevitable. Like he was setting me up.

He would tell me not to bring my purse because I would just lose it anyway. So I left it at home.

My ID. My credit cards. Everything.

I didn't question him because he was right.

I did leave things behind. ADHD will do that to you. I appreciated that he would be responsible for everything. I didn't need anything else.

I tried to bring my purse once. After the second time he left me somewhere.

He didn't like it.

I got a new dress after that one.

This is how it went for the first three years.

But the cruise was different. Seven days in the Caribbean Sea.

He always seemed better on vacations. It affirmed what he said: stress was the problem.

On the cruise, he was happy. Lighter. Like the air had returned to his lungs. Like the fog had lifted.

We made friends with our tablemates. They were nice. Older. They shared their duty-free Johnnie Walker Blue Label whiskey with us.

We gambled. He taught me blackjack. We danced at the club. He was a terrible dancer. But on vacation, he didn't care.

On our sea days, we had drinks by the pool. Peach in color, taste of pineapple. I loved them. They went down easily.

We docked in the British Virgin Islands for the day. We went on an excursion in the morning. The Baths of Tortola. Gray rock formations. Turquoise water. I jumped off a cliff. Dropped straight and deep into the water. Like a weighted pencil.

After the excursion, we walked around town, looking for a place to eat. He wanted a sit-down restaurant. He told me to pick one.

I didn't care. I said so.

My apathy bothered him. He said I was acting ungrateful.

I wasn't trying to be difficult. I was trying to be accommodating.

He got mad at me for being indecisive. Told me not to be stupid. "Just make a decision."

It felt like there was a right answer. I just didn't know what it was.

We were walking down the street. People everywhere.

He raised his voice but kept it controlled. Only a few people stopped to look.

He insisted I pick a place.

I told him I didn't know one. That there were places all around us. I said any of them would be fine. That I could always find something on a menu.

But I didn't give a definitive answer. I didn't make a decision.

That was my mistake.

He got angry and walked away. Didn't say a word. Just turned around and disappeared.

Multiple cruise ships had ported that day and brought droves of people with them. I saw him in the crowd. Tried to catch up.

I walked quickly, weaving in and out of people. I stepped out of my flip-flop. Looked down to put it back on.

When I looked up, he was gone.

I stood there. On a street in the British Virgin Islands. Wearing a bikini and a pair of running shorts.

No phone. No ID. No money.

Nothing.

I didn't have a way to get back on the ship. My cruise card—my ticket back on board—was in his wallet.

I didn't know what to do.

I started panicking. Everything became blurry. I couldn't breathe. I stepped off the street into an alley. Sat down on the ground. My back pressed against a pink wall. Tears fell freely.

I couldn't stop crying.

It wasn't the first time he left me. But this time was different. I didn't know how to get home.

I don't know how long I sat there. Long enough that a woman stopped to check on me.

I didn't tell her what happened. Just that I needed to get back to the ship.

She gave me directions.

When I saw the ship, I inhaled for the first deep time since he left. I thought I was safe.

But the crew member at the ramp asked for my card. I told her I didn't have it. That it was with him.

She told me I couldn't board without it.

I was still shaking. Eyes puffy. Fighting back another round of tears.

She could tell something was off. Her voice softened.

She said she could call the American consulate for me. They could help me get back home. I wouldn't need my cruise card. I wouldn't need him. They could verify who I was. They could get me out of this mess.

I told her I would think about it. But I knew I wouldn't.

I was afraid of what waited for me if I did.

I stayed at the dock. I knew when everyone had to be back on board. 5:00 p.m.

He had to come back.

I sat there for hours.
Scratched at my thumbnails until they bled.

I watched families board. Watched couples. Sunburned tourists. Laughing children.

I watched everyone return to something. With every minute that passed, I felt more and more like nothing.

He walked up to the ship a little after 4:00. Casual. Like nothing had happened. Like he was just another guy on vacation.

He saw me sitting at a table by the dock. Walked over. Calm.

"There you are," he said. "I wondered if you'd be here or if you'd still be frozen in the street, trying to make a decision about what to eat."

He was making a joke.

"I'm glad you made the smart choice."

I told him I was glad too. And I meant it.

We walked up the silver ramp to the ship. The same crew member from before asked for our cruise cards. He handed her both.

She scanned them. Handed them back. Looked him in the eye.

And glared.

I don't think he caught it. But I did.

I also caught her name. Right there on her silver name tag.

Mariah. From Dallas.

I'll never forget it.

Back on the ship, it was time to get ready for dinner. I expected him to say something. To acknowledge that what he did was fucked up. To follow the script. The one he had used so many times before.

But he didn't.

He didn't say anything.

He asked me which shirt he should wear.

I didn't feel like going to dinner. I wasn't hungry.

He didn't care. He didn't want to be embarrassed in front of our tablemates. He wanted them to like him.

He told me I was going to dinner. So I better get dressed.

So I did.

That night was a blur. I sat at dinner, wondering how two worlds could exist at the same time.

One where we were laughing. Telling stories. Like life was fun.

The other, more sinister. Where he wasn't the good guy.

Or maybe he was.

Maybe he was right. Maybe my mother was right. Maybe my dad was right.

Maybe I was the problem. Maybe this was just how people loved me.

The next day, we went to the U.S. Virgin Islands. He must have felt bad about leaving me in Tortola.

He bought me a Tag Heuer watch.

Almost $1,000.

I barely wore it.

Dried Drops of Drool

By the time we moved back to our home state, he controlled everything.

What we did. What I said. Who I was friends with. What I wore. What I ate.

He would make comments about not wanting a fat wife. He told me when I could order dessert. When I couldn't.

He said he wanted a wife who met him at the door. A drink in her hand. Wearing a skirt.

So that's what I did.

Not because I wanted to. But because I didn't have a choice. At least, it didn't feel that way.

I had no money. None that was mine.

I didn't have a job. I didn't have friends. I didn't have a support system.

And I certainly didn't have my family.

My mother and I were barely speaking. I was estranged from my dad.

My sister, Robynn, and I talked some. But I never felt safe enough to tell her what was going on.

I was in his world.

His family. His friends. His needs.

All of it belonged to him.

So did I.

I've wondered thousands of times why I didn't leave. Maybe more.

I didn't know where I would go. I didn't know what I would do.

I always thought isolation was the reason. That I never left because I didn't have anyone else.

But now, I'm not so sure.

Part of me felt I deserved that treatment. That I deserved to be called stupid. I deserved it when he put his hands on me, when he left me somewhere.

I deserved my gilded cage.

I used to remind myself how lucky I was.

I didn't have to worry about bills. Or pay rent. Or wonder how the lights would stay on.

I just had to survive in his world. Keep him happy.

I just had to disappear a little more each day.

I didn't care until we had a baby on the way. I started taking better care of myself. I improved my diet. I tried to get enough sleep.

At night, I lay awake worrying. Playing out scenarios in my mind.

It was one thing for him to hurt me. It was something else entirely to think about him hurting our child.

That thought kept me up at night.

He was kinder to me when I was pregnant. So excited to be a dad. His face lit up when he talked about it.

I didn't have an easy pregnancy. Not because of him or the baby. My body wasn't built for it. My autoimmune condition made everything harder.

But when I held my sweet, perfect, gorgeous son, I felt a flicker of something inside me.

Hope.

Hope that now things would change. Hope that the cycles would break. Hope that everything would be okay.

For a while, it was.

He relished being a dad. He was good at it.

Patient. Helpful. Loving.

I really thought we had turned a corner. I thought the past would stay in the past. I thought the cycles were over.

They weren't.

Nine months.

That's how long I made it before I messed up.

That's how long he made it before punishing me.

Our son was sleeping in my arms. I was rocking him in the nursery. Singing "Baby Mine" from *Dumbo*.

He came into the room. Knelt beside the recliner.

My arm was on the armrest, its tan suede fabric starting to wear—just a little. Getting smooth. Like a newly broken-in shoe. Just starting to find its stride.

He rested his head on my palm. His chin pressed downward.

I held his head in my hand.

It was heavy.

He thought I was pushing back on him. Like I was resisting.

He said it was hurting his neck.

I tried to tell him I didn't mean to.

Before I could finish speaking, he grabbed me by the throat.

His hands wrapped around my neck. He asked me how I liked it. If I enjoyed being pressed on like that.

I squeaked that I didn't.

He squeezed harder.

One final reminder that he was in charge.

And then he let go.

I immediately got up from the chair. Brought my son into our bedroom. Closed the door and locked it.

I looked in the mirror.

The red marks on my neck looked back at me.

Like five hot dogs.

They just needed a bun.

He didn't yell. He didn't bang on the door.

His parents were at our house. He didn't want them to see who he really was.

He could control it: The anger. The violence. The abuse.

He just didn't control it around me.

His voice was low and steady. Measured.

He mocked me.

Said that at some point, I'd learn. Or maybe not.

I stood there.

My son in my arms. The red marks still burned on my neck.

He was already laughing. Already walking away. Already certain I would stay.

He had every reason to believe I would.

Because I always had.

But this time?

This time, something was different.

I saw it.

He didn't.

Not yet.

I wondered if he would.

I looked down at my son: Still sleeping. Tiny drops of dried drool at the corner of his mouth.

I held him tighter. Snuggled him into my chest. Kissed the top of his head. The faint smell of his baby shampoo tickled my nostrils.

And something clicked.

Finally.

I knew if I stayed and my child grew up in this environment, he could be just like his dad.

My baby might grow up thinking this was okay.

Or he might not.

Would he see me as weak?

Would he be disappointed that he didn't have a mother who fought back?

I knew my baby deserved better.

So right there. In my bedroom. Behind a locked door. Holding my infant son.

I made a plan to leave.

I made a plan to get out.

- -

"I'm sorry."

I turn in the direction of her voice. It's small. Unsteady.

"Why are you apologizing, 20s Me?"

I genuinely don't know.

"My voice was shaking the whole time. It still is."

She sounds disappointed. Like she expected something different. Like she expected *herself* to be different.

"Why is that a problem?" I ask, keeping my tone steady.
"You were sharing something terrifying.
Something hard.
It makes sense that your voice would shake."

She doesn't answer right away. I know what she's doing. I wait for her.

"I just…thought I would be better.
I thought I would be stronger for you.
I'm not."

My heart sinks. She doesn't see it. She doesn't see the strength isn't in *how* she told her story.

It's the fact that she *did*.

I exhale carefully. I know how much she hates compliments. If I'm not mindful, she'll slip further back into the darkness. And I won't be able to find her for a while.

"20s Me, I am not disappointed in you."
I pause, measuring my words.
"It's the opposite, actually.
I am so deeply proud of you."

Silence.

She's waiting for the catch. The *but* that, this time, will never come.

I take another breath and continue.

"You did it right.
Your job was to survive, and you did.

It wasn't easy.
It wasn't pretty.
But you made it.
And because you did, I can be here with you now."

Her breath hitches. I hear it. I feel it.

"By surviving, you didn't just save yourself.
You saved me, too.
And every version of me that comes after."

"At what cost?"

Her voice is louder now. But it's still trembling.

An uneasy feeling washes over me. One I know too well.

Shame.

She feels it too. It wraps around her like a second skin.

"You know what's next." Her voice is quieter now. Fractured. *"You know where we're going. You know what I did."*

I hear her sniffling. The tears must have started falling, but she's still in the shadows. Still hiding.

I inhale. Exhale. Keep my voice steady.

"I do.
I know what comes next.
I know it's hard."

I pause. She doesn't say anything. Just more sniffles.

I take a step closer to the dark.

"I also know something else."

She stills. I can feel her watching me now.

"I know you are capable.
I know you are confident.
And I know you are brave."

She doesn't move.

I reach for her anyway.

"You can do this.
I will be right here with you.
Every step of the way."

And then—

A breath.

Hers.

Mine.

One shared moment in the dark.

She doesn't step forward. Not yet.

But she doesn't disappear either.

And for now, that's enough.

7.

Haunted

20s Me stays in the darkness.

But I know she's still here.

I can hear her breathing. Shallow. Uneven.

I can hear her sniffling.

I can *feel* her.

Like static in the air. Like a presence pressing against my awareness.

I don't move toward her. I don't try to pull her out.

I just sit.

"There's no rush."
My voice is soft, steady.
"We don't have to keep going if you're not ready.
You don't have to be."

More sniffles.

A shuddering breath.

Still, she doesn't move.

I stay quiet. Let the moment settle. Hold space for her without expectation.

Minutes pass. Maybe longer.

The silence stretches, thick and heavy. Like a weighted blanket over my chest.

I wonder if she's disappeared again. If she's slipped further into the dark.

I'm about to let her go—

then, a voice.

Fragile. Small.

"Let's keep going."

I hesitate.

"Are you sure?"

She doesn't answer right away.

I wait.

"We don't have to," I offer.

Another pause.

Then—

"I can't keep hiding."

Her voice cracks.

"I have to own my shit."

I exhale, grounding myself. I settle in.

I don't tell her how proud I am. Not yet. She wouldn't believe me anyway.

She takes a breath.

It's ragged.

Unsteady.

Just like her.

Andrew Jackson

I kept it to myself—my decision to leave him.
I knew I couldn't do anything to trip his alarm bells. It would be bad for me if I did.

I made small changes. I started taking an extra $20 in cash when I went to Target or the grocery store.

Just $20.

Nothing that would look suspicious. He didn't know how much things cost, so he wouldn't ask questions. $20 wouldn't be noticeable, and I could do it every time.

So I did.

Each ding of the cash register was a step closer to safety. Every bill felt like a heartbeat toward freedom.

Each time, it felt like a quiet little rebellion. One hundred and four small ways of calling back my power.

$20.

$20.

$20.

Every week for 104 weeks. Deposited into my own bank account. One he didn't know about.

I snuck whatever extra I could, whenever I could. Little by little, I saved a few thousand.

I was patient. I was persistent.

And I never missed a Target run.

Trash

It took a little over two years.

During that time, our marriage got progressively worse.

I stopped caring. I checked out. I didn't want to pretend anymore.

I knew I was leaving. I just wanted to go. It agonized me to stay.

Like being in two places at once. My mind was already gone. My body just needed to catch up.

He noticed a change in me, and he didn't like it.

He still yelled at me. Still got frustrated. But he didn't put his hands on me anymore.

Not after he choked me.

It did something to him. Like he saw something in himself he didn't like.

When he drank, he often became that person. His drinking usually meant I was going to get yelled at. Or have things thrown at me. Or worse.

But now it was different. He stopped being violent.

Instead, he got hysterical. His voice rose in pitch.
He talked faster, wandered off. He would literally walk out the front door and keep going.

No idea where he was headed. Usually no phone.

He got drunk at my son's first birthday party. We had family over to celebrate.

Near the end of the party, I heard it.

The high-pitched voice.

I knew what was coming.

When he talked in that voice, it always made me think of Judge Doom in *Who Framed Roger Rabbit?* The way his voice shrieked, his eyes bulging during the film's climax..

That part always scared me as a kid.

It scared me at the party, too.

His dad and I were cleaning up decorations.

He came in from outside. His voice shrieking.

His dad told him to knock it off.

He listened. Got quiet.

Then he went back outside.

And disappeared.

Left without saying a word.

An hour passed. I called his phone. No answer.

I wasn't worried. I wasn't anything.

I took the trash out to the dumpster in the alley.

And there he was.

Sitting by the dumpster. Budweisers in his lap.

He said he walked up to the liquor store. Bought some beer. Didn't want to come inside because he knew I'd be mad. So he sat there. Drinking alone.

Ashamed to be drunk on my son's first birthday.

I looked at him with disgust. Threw the trash in the dumpster. And walked back inside.

He was right where he needed to be.

Chinese Food

I started drinking more at night. Numbing the pain. Just like him.

I went back to college. A second undergraduate degree. Still trying to prove I wasn't stupid.

That's where I met Katherine.

She was funny. Her humor and energy matched mine. Like she had seen darkness, too. And could still laugh about it.

She was the first real friend I'd had in years.

He hated her.

He saw her as competition. He would power-call me when I was out with her, demanding I come home. He raged because I stopped listening to him. I didn't care.

Every act of defiance made me feel stronger. Like I was cracking out of the shell I had been living in.

It took one person. One real friendship.

Katherine was the crack in the door where air gets in.

As time wore on, I stopped even trying to keep up appearances. I stopped caring. I became depressed. Functional, but emotionally withdrawn.

I think he could sense my growing apathy. He tried to give me back some of my life. Released some of the control. He let me go out with my new friends from college. People he didn't know. Some were men.

It looked like growth. Like he was really trying. Maybe to him, it felt like progress.

But it wasn't.

It was just control in a different form.

He couldn't just let me enjoy my time. He would power-call. Dozens of times. Long voicemails that vacillated between anger and tears.

Anger: insulting me as a mother.

Tears: telling me I was a wonderful mother.

Anger: calling me a colossal bitch.

Tears: telling me he was so lucky to have me.

It was so desperate. I could see through it. Through all of it. I could see the manipulation.

And it happened all the time.

Case in point: my birthday.

I wanted Chinese food. He had it for lunch and didn't want it again.

But it was my birthday. And it was what I wanted.

His mom watched our son. We got in the car. Sat in silence.

He drove us. Told me to pick somewhere else. Anywhere else.

Just not Chinese.

But that's what I wanted. I told him so.

He screamed at me in the car.

It hurt my ears. I gripped the seat, bracing for what was next.

For the yelling, for the slamming, for whatever this was going to be.

But before I could react—

he threw the car into park. Opened the door. And walked into the middle of a busy street.

Cars swerved past. Honking. There was someone behind us.

Cars whizzed by on my right. I had to wait for them to stop before I could open the door. I got out of the car and ran around to the driver's seat. I didn't even bother moving the seat forward. I put the car in drive. And turned around at the first chance I got.

I saw him. Standing on the sidewalk.

For half a second, I wanted to keep driving. Leave him behind. Abandon him and our history.

A small part of me wanted to drive up onto the curb.

To hit him.

I knew I wouldn't. But I won't lie and say I didn't enjoy the thought.

I had a million reasons to drive past him that day. But reasons don't pay rent. Reasons don't buy food. Reasons don't keep you safe.

I slowed down.

I knew I couldn't leave yet. I needed more time. More money.

And so I continued to play my part.

I knew I had to pick him up. I couldn't just let him walk. We had to go home together.

But I was so sick of his shit.

I wanted him to sit under the weight of his selfishness. Walking into traffic. Leaving me parked in the middle of the street.

I rolled down the passenger-side window. Told him I was parking in a nearby lot.

He met me there.

Already hysterical. Talking rapidly. High-pitched voice. Bulging eyes.

Judge Doom.

My stomach dropped. Fear radiated through me. My hands gripped the wheel. My knuckles turned white.

I was scared. I wanted to stand up for myself. I knew I could.

I used my mantra.

I am capable. I am confident. I am brave.
I am capable. I am confident. I am brave.
I am capable. I am confident. I am brave.

I took a deep breath. And then another.

I calmly told him to get in the car.

I calmly told him we were going home.

I calmly told him I had lost my appetite.

He started to panic. His voice quickened.

My body tensed tighter.

He got louder.

His arms reached through the window. He started banging on the inside of the car.

My breath stopped. Time stopped.

I waited for it.

The sound of his hand across my face. Or against the back of my head. Punishment for my defiance.

It never came.

He told me we were going to get Chinese food. Told me he didn't want to ruin the night. Begged me to go to dinner. Told me he felt guilty.

It was so confusing.

Why now? Why feel guilty now?

Does he know I'm leaving? Does he know my plan?

I didn't want to go to dinner. But I didn't know what to do.

Will he hurt me if I don't go? Will he hurt me if I don't pretend to have a good time? Do I care?

Will it hurt him if I don't go to dinner? Will it hurt him if he knew I didn't want to? Do I care?

I told him the truth.

I didn't want to have dinner with him. I didn't want to spend my time or energy on him that night.

My breath—and time—stopped. I could hear my heartbeat. Fast.

And then it happened.

For the first time, I saw fear on his face.

He knew I was approaching a breaking point. He knew I was becoming strong enough to leave.

Without saying a word, I knew.

I won that round.

I knew it wouldn't last. But I had defied him, and the world didn't end.

It wouldn't be the last fight. But for the first time, I felt like I had a chance.

Truffle Oil

The next day, he took me to the fancy mall. The one with the high-end stores. He told me to pick out a new purse.

I told him I didn't want one.

He begged me to pick one, desperation in his voice. He needed to buy me something to absolve himself.

I picked the first one I saw in the store. A silk Coach purse. $800.

That night, I took it with me to the art museum. I sat in the parking lot. About to go in and tour the museum with my friends.

Thirty-seven times.

That's how many times he called while I was driving there.

Thirty-seven missed calls. In eighteen minutes.

I decided to leave my phone in the car. I didn't want to deal with him.

Before I did, I answered his thirty-eighth call.

I told him I wanted a night with my friends.

He begged me to come home. For a redo of my birthday.

He begged to go get Chinese food.

I told him no. To stop calling me. That I wanted to enjoy my night.

And then, I put my phone in the console and went to meet my friends.

When I left the museum two hours later, there were *eighty-one missed calls.*

He desperately grasped for control. Like a drowning man in search of air. Flailing.

But he had stopped calling. Finally. I guess he realized I was serious.

I went to dinner at a nice restaurant with my friends after the art museum.

I got a little tipsy. I accidentally spilled truffle oil on my new silk purse.

The cleaners said there was nothing they could do. The stain was permanent.

I wasn't sad. I didn't even care.

I threw the purse in the dumpster with the rest of the trash.

Retention Package

Every day, I wanted out.

Out of that marriage. Out of that life.

I dreamt about it.

Not about some big, sweeping, dramatic change—just small things. I dreamt about grocery shopping alone without getting twenty missed calls. About sitting on the couch in silence without feeling like I rested on eggshells. About reading a book in bed without worrying about what mood he'd come home in. Making dinner without having to guess what he wanted before he even said it.

I didn't dream about running away or starting over somewhere far away. I just dreamt about peace.

At the same time, I was numb. I didn't let anything in. Good or bad. Not close enough to feel.

I would think about hopeful scenarios. But I wouldn't feel hopeful. Nothing got past the armor.

Except for my son.

His laugh. His mischievous smile. The way the world was magic to him. The way he was magic to me.

An anxious anticipation hummed through my body. Anxiety for the number of changes coming. For the unknowns.

Anxiety for how he would react. How it would affect my son.

Anticipation for a life that would truly be mine.

I was twenty-eight years old, and I was going to be in charge of my life for the first time ever. I felt terrified and nearly free. What I imagine base jumping probably feels like. Adrenaline coursing through my veins.

A secret I knew, but no one else did. A growing impatience. Every day felt like a prison sentence.

Endlessly long. Emotionally heavy.

He slept in the basement.

We barely spoke.

He could sense what was coming. I must not have been hiding it as well as I thought.

In early December, he made me an offer. More of a *Please-Don't-Divorce-Me* package.

A *Marital Retention Package*:
- My dream vacation to Iceland
- A $5,000 shopping spree
- A Vespa scooter

He saw it as a cheaper alternative to losing half of everything.

I told him no. That I wasn't interested in his package.

I asked for practical things for Christmas. A new set of kitchen knives. Expensive pots and pans.

Things I would use in my new life.

I normally didn't ask for much at Christmas. I wasn't a *stuff* person.

But that year, I was.

He got it all for me. I still don't know if he realized what I was doing. But suddenly, I had fewer things to buy for my new life.

Shortly after Christmas, we went on vacation. He wanted to go skiing.

We spent the trip separately. Each doing our own thing.

He skied the blue runs.

I played in the snow with my son. We built a snowman in the park.

We went to a cheese store and ate samples. My son laughed after every bite. Like he thought he was getting away with something.

We went to the same small restaurant every morning for breakfast. Right in the heart of town. Only a few tables and a counter.

I had oatmeal. My son ate scrambled eggs and toast with mixed berry jam.

On our last day, the server gave us a jar of jam for free. She saw how much he loved it.

That server. That jam. That week on vacation.

It all gave me the confidence to know my son and I would be okay.

I can't really explain why. Maybe because I could navigate time alone with my son in a space we had never been. I could do it on my own.

We could have normalcy.

It was an important piece of the puzzle. An unknown but vital piece of the escape plan.

Once that piece clicked into place, things moved quickly.

Less than a month after that trip, I signed a lease on a new apartment.

I signed the lease on a Tuesday in early February. The ground was frozen. The trees, bare. No snow, just the dull, gray residue of winter. The time of year when everything is cold and dirty, when the world feels stuck, waiting for the thaw. Waiting for spring. Waiting for re-birth.

My apartment was on the second floor of a four-family flat. I had an off-street parking space, two bedrooms, and one bathroom. 900 square feet of freedom.

He somehow knew something was up.

He called while I was at the leasing office. I had already signed the lease, handed over the security deposit, and paid the pet deposit for Bailey. I didn't answer when he called.

His voicemail waited for me as I walked out of the office. His voice was small, hesitant. He asked if I was getting an apartment. How did he know? Was he following me? Did he have someone else watching me? Was it just a lucky guess? I still don't know. But it spooked me.

I held the apartment keys in my hand, the metal still cold from the leasing agent's desk.

I drove to the new place, checking my rearview mirror at every stop-light, convinced I was being followed.

I don't think I was. But I don't know for sure.

I unlocked the door and stepped inside. I stood in the living room, picturing where the furniture could go.

The couch against the far wall. The bookshelf tucked in the corner. Would the chair be too tall for the front window? Bailey loved looking outside. I didn't want to take that away from him.

I walked into my son's bedroom, imagining his tiny toddler bed against the far wall: His clothes hanging neatly in the closet. His toys scattered on the floor. I could almost hear his giggles, the sound of his feet padding across the hardwood.

I stood in my new bedroom. The walls were bright white, the trim a warm, natural wood. The room was small, but to me it felt enormous.

Will I sleep better here? Will the constant worrying and planning finally stop? Will the flashbacks?

In the kitchen, I ran my hand over the countertop. I imagined making meals for my son, pulling chicken nuggets from the oven, pouring a cup of coffee while he played in the next room.

I could see myself curled up on the couch with a book. I could see my life here, a life that was finally mine.

It didn't feel suffocating. It didn't feel claustrophobic. It didn't feel heavy.

There were no bad memories here. No fights. No yelling. No one calling me stupid. No more messing up.

It felt lighter here. I felt lighter.

I knew what was coming. I would have to tell him. I had a plan for that, too.

World Map

I didn't say anything to him when he got home from work. I waited until after I put my son to bed.

He didn't say much when I told him about the apartment, like he had been expecting it. He sat there, quiet for a while.

Is he processing? Planning revenge? I didn't know, but the longer the silence stretched, the more nervous I became.

Then, he started to cry.

He looked so defeated, as if having power over me had been his life force, and now, I was draining it from him. Calling it back to me.

But he wasn't mad.

He was sad.

Not about losing me. He was mourning the loss of the façade. The image of our perfect life. The way he would have to explain it to everyone he knew.

We were separating.

I knew we were getting a divorce, but he begged me not to say it. Begged me to be open to all possibilities. He told me he didn't want to feel like a failure.

I thought it was interesting that he didn't feel like one before.

I told him I had rented a U-Haul and would be picking it up on Friday.

He asked who was helping me move.

I told him I asked his best friend and Katherine, the only two people who knew the truth about our marriage. The only ones who knew about our troubles.

He offered to increase my *Please-Don't-Divorce-Me* package.

He would take me anywhere in the world I wanted to go—in addition to Iceland.

He offered me more money. A nicer car.

I didn't even have to say no. He already knew.

He said he thought I was only leaving now because his stepdad had died. That Jim was the only reason I had stayed.

I did love his stepdad.

He was kind to me. Always. He had a twinkle in his eye, like a real-life Santa Claus.

Jim loved my son. He never had biological kids of his own, so being a grandpa meant everything to him. When he held my son, that twinkle shone even brighter. A special magic sparkled between those two, and it extinguished too soon.

Jim died when my son was eight months old. It shattered my heart.

But Jim's death wasn't why I left.

Katherine helped me pick up a couch and chair I bought on Craigslist. She bought me towels—orange ones—to match a shower curtain I had picked out.

My life was coming together. I watched it happen; it unfolded in front of me.

I felt terrified, but also excited.

I had never lived on my own before. Never paid an electric bill. Or a credit card bill. Or rent.

I was a mother, and I was learning how to be an adult for the first time.

I asked Katherine's opinion on everything. I didn't want to make the wrong choice.

For the first time in my life, I got to choose things for myself. And yet, every decision felt like a test. Like there was a right answer I was supposed to know. Like I should already have preferences, opinions.

"What color curtains do you want?"

"What kind of rug would look nice?"

I had no idea. And, honestly, I didn't care.

Katherine wanted me to have a space that felt like my own. A place that was pretty.

But even the smallest questions overwhelmed me.

"Do you like this throw pillow or that throw pillow?"

It felt like a trick.

Like I would somehow mess up. Like I would somehow get hurt.

I didn't know what kind of throw pillow I liked. Or what type of plates I wanted. I had never had time to think about those things. They had always seemed so small, so insignificant.

But my son's room mattered.

I needed it to feel like home.

I hung a map on the wall, right by his bed. I would use it to teach him geography.

We would pick a place on the map, look at pictures of it online, and then we would meet there in our dreams. I would call them our dream dates.

A way for us to be together.

Even when we had to be apart.

I knew leaving meant freedom. But it would also cost me time with my son.

I knew my choice would hurt him. I knew a divorce would alter his life. That he would suffer consequences for something he didn't choose. That his childhood would be collateral damage.

I needed his room to be just right. I needed him to feel safe. I needed it to feel different.

Maybe then he would understand why I left.

Dr. Dumb-Dumb

It felt like a dream.

I kept expecting to wake up back in the life where I had no choices. Where my safety depended on his happiness.

Instead, it was moving day.

We loaded the U-Haul quickly. I didn't have much to take.

I never looked back when we drove away from the house. I sat in the passenger seat, staring straight ahead, but I could see him out of the corner of my eye. Standing in the doorway. Watching me through the glass.

I refused to look at him. But I made sure to smile.

After we got everything into the apartment, his best friend left. Katherine stayed. We unpacked several boxes. Eventually, she left, too.

I closed the front door. Locked it.

Then I pushed the couch in front of it.

It was the only way I could sleep.

I did it every night for the first two weeks. Until he started dating someone else.

The first few days in the apartment blurred past. But the nights moved slowly, stretching time just to hold me in the darkness. I always felt anxious for the daylight to come. It never came fast enough.

Daytime meant distractions.

I had my son every two days. We had a two-two-three arrangement—every Monday and Tuesday, and every other weekend.

On the nights I didn't have him, I felt jumpier.

The quiet in the apartment stretched and grew like something was waiting for me.

I would lay in bed, staring at the ceiling. The silence pressed in around me. No screaming. No tension. Just me and my thoughts.

It was unsettling.

I had gotten so used to the chaos that peace felt unnatural.

I tossed and turned, pulling the blanket tighter.

Every night, I looked for my monsters. I opened every closet door. Looked under the beds. Checked the windows. Nothing.

That was somehow worse than something.

I kept looking for a reason to feel afraid.

Something to make the fear inside me make sense.

My stomach stayed in knots.

Shouldn't I be relieved? Shouldn't I feel free? Shouldn't I feel safe?

Instead, I felt more on edge. Like something was coming to get me.

A feeling of impending doom.

But what was it?

My body would tense for no reason. Outside noises sent shivers down my spine. My neighbor, Ellen, coming home made my heart race. The sound of someone in the hallway—footsteps, a shuffle—made me hold my breath.

Then, Ellen's door would open and close.

I would breathe again.

I always checked over my shoulder, wondering if I would see him. If I would feel him before I did.

My mind kept making plans.

Preparations for when it all fell apart.

I couldn't let myself stay there too long.

I had to keep moving forward.

I had to keep going.

I had to learn to survive in this new world.

The flashbacks started about three weeks after I moved out.

They came at all times. In unexpected ways.

I would be playing Magna-Tiles with my son, and the sharp clap of the tiles snapping together sounded just like his hand across my face.

The smell of roasted turkey from Boston Market reminded me of when he threw turkey at me, furious we weren't having roast beef.

But then, there were other moments.

Moments where my breath flowed more easily.

Like sitting on my fire escape, talking to Ellen.

She was from New York and sounded like it. She was in her seventies and took care of her sick husband.

She loved Bailey. She loved me. She loved my son.

But she hated him.

She called him *Dr. Dumb-Dumb.*

It always made me giggle.

Such a childish name.

But she said it with such vitriol, like it was a curse.

That always made me laugh harder.

She would bring me dinner, insisting she had made too much.

I knew better.

Alimony

I saw him every two days for handoff. He was happy. Dating someone new.

He would call on my nights to talk to my son. Said he had something to ask me about him. But really, he just wanted to tell me about *her*. Like I was his friend.

He would tell me he felt guilty. That he missed me. That if I just said the word, he'd break up with her. Like I would want him back.

I didn't care. I didn't engage. I made excuses to get off the phone.

I didn't want to know about his life. I didn't need anything else tethering me to him.

About a month after I moved out, he brought up the divorce. Said he would handle everything. He would petition the court.

He asked to do it without lawyers. It would be faster that way. Cleaner. Cheaper. I agreed.

I didn't want to fight. I didn't have any fight left in me. I didn't want a long, drawn-out process. I just needed it to be over.

He asked for 50-50 custody. I had read that it was the most favored option for kids. The one that did the least amount of damage. Allowed a child to have a relationship with both parents. I agreed.

I turned down alimony.

I had almost no money. I could have used it. *Should* have used it. Katherine thought I was crazy. Said I wasn't looking out for myself.

She didn't understand. This wasn't about the money. I refused to let him have that power over me.

Alimony meant he would tell me I was only making it on my own because of him. I didn't have to wonder if he would. I *knew* it.

I knew he would throw it in my face whenever he got the chance.

He could hold alimony over me.

He didn't get to claim my new life. I wouldn't let him. Even if it cost me.

He submitted the paperwork to the state. We would go to the courthouse in May.

I ran through my savings quickly. I had almost nothing.

I could have gotten a minimum-wage job. Worked retail. Or in a restaurant. But I didn't.

A Google search gave me another option.

You can't remove access to joint accounts during a divorce. Courts don't like it.

I told him this. He already knew. I think he was hoping I wouldn't find out.

I told him it was my money too. At least until everything was finalized.

I told him I was staying home with my son. I would go back to teaching when he started preschool in August. Just three months after our court date.

I told him I wouldn't make enough to pay for daycare otherwise.

He agreed it didn't make sense for such a short period of time.

He wrote me a check each month for child support. He included extra until I started my teaching job.

Three months. That's how long he paid extra.

Was that alimony? Did I betray myself from the beginning?

I still don't know.

During that time, he frequently reminded me he was paying for my new life.

God. He was so fucking predictable.

Ick

I was always holding my breath. I could never escape him.

Not fully.

I didn't have to deal with physical violence anymore. I didn't have to endure him calling me stupid anymore. But I still had to see him. I had to coparent with him. I had to be *nice.*

We went to breakfast every Sunday. The three of us. It was when we did handoffs from the weekend. I wanted my son to see his parents get along. I wanted my divorce to feel different than my parents' divorce.

I never got to take my armor off, because he was still there. Even when he wasn't.

He was in my mind. The flashbacks playing on repeat.

He was in my ear. His voice echoing from my memories. As though he were right behind me. Whispering.

Stupid. Stupid. Stupid.

He was in my nervous system.

My legs would sometimes shake when I knew he was coming to pick up my son. My palms would sweat when I walked my son to his truck. My body would go rigid if he bumped into me.

He wasn't in my home anymore. But he was in the way my breath hitched when my phone rang. In the way I flinched when someone reached for something near me. In the way I could never, ever fully relax my shoulders.

He wasn't living with me anymore, but he was living *inside* me.

The damage he had done showed up in my everyday life. Like runoff from a sewage plant. Thick and gooey. The sludge of his actions coating my insides. Suffocating me from within.

It was as if I was drowning just under the surface. My lungs were full of air. But my body was waiting for the next wave to take me back under.

Indecision paralyzed me. I didn't know the right answer. I didn't have anyone's actions to read. No one to tiptoe around. No one to make happy. To keep happy.

My mind scrambled, looking for a familiar pattern.

There wasn't one.

I didn't know who I was. I didn't know how to act. I operated like everyone was a danger. A threat.

I was always aware. I was always on guard.

My perfectionism worsened. My masking improved.

I was a chameleon. A different version of myself for every person. Perfectly blending in with what made them comfortable. I never let my outside show what was happening on the inside.

That's what kept me safe.

From others.

But not from myself.

My Greatest Shame

I can name the specific moment.

The one that haunts me. The one that clings to me like thick, wet fabric—drenched in regret, heavy with shame.

A decision I made out of fear and exhaustion. A decision I will never forgive myself for.

May came.

We went to the courthouse to stand in front of the judge and have him sign off on our divorce.

We had to get there early, and we had to wait our turn.

I was standing outside the courtroom when a sheriff approached me. His expression was unreadable.

"Are you Megan?"

I nodded.

"The judge wants to see you."

My stomach clenched. The world around me went sharp, too clear. I followed the sheriff into the courtroom, each step feeling heavier than the last.

An older man with dark hair and round glasses, the judge, sat behind his bench. His voice was gruff, but not unkind.

He didn't look at me the way other men in authority had. He wasn't assessing. He wasn't amused. He was…concerned.

"I've been looking over your divorce agreement," he said, flipping through the papers. "And I have some questions."

I could hear my pulse in my ears.

"It's highly unfavorable to you," he continued, adjusting his glasses. "I see you've waived alimony. Why?"

"I don't want it," I answered quickly. Too quickly.

He raised his eyebrows. "Are you okay? Are you safe?"

I slowed my breath.

"I'm okay."

The judge scanned my face. I adjusted it so he wouldn't see anything.

"What about custody?" He looked at me over the rim of his glasses. "Courts tend to favor keeping a child under five with their mother. Are you sure this arrangement is what's best?"

My breath caught.

"I am not trying to tell you what to do, I just need to make sure you understand. You don't have a lawyer, and if you want, you can stop these proceedings today. You can get an attorney. You can fight this."

His words hung in the air, thick and suffocating.

I was already thinking about it.

Thinking about how angry *he* got. How much he loved a fight. How it lit something up inside him—something dark. Sinister.

Thinking about money. How I had barely $100 in my bank account. How I was living off his money, the same money that could be used to crush me in court.

Thinking about his unpredictability. The way he could twist a situation. The way he could make me the villain.

Thinking about how tired I was.

The judge waited. The sheriff waited.

I swallowed hard.

I tried to picture it—saying no. Stopping this. Fighting.

I tried to picture the hearings. The lawyer fees. The hours in court. The look on his face when he realized I was trying to take our son.

I pictured the rage. The consequences. The battle that would never end.

I pictured my son in the middle of it.

My stomach twisted so violently I thought I might throw up right there in front of the judge.

I looked down at my hands. They were trembling.

"Um…I think—" I stopped myself.

"*No,*" I insisted. My voice was small. Weak. "I want to keep the agreement."

The judge studied me for a moment. His lips pressed together, holding something back.

Then he nodded.

"Alright."

That was it.

He looked back down at his stack of paperwork. A pile of other up-ending marriages.

I left the courtroom with the sheriff. We went before the judge less than thirty minutes later.

It was done.

I was divorced.

I should have felt free.

Instead, my stomach dropped—like a free-fall, like stepping off the edge of something I could never climb back up.

I had taken the only out I had.

But I hadn't taken it for both of us.

I took it for me.

I knew who he was. I knew what he was capable of.

And I let him have my son 50 percent of the time.

20s Me stops talking.

The silence between us is thick, suffocating. The weight of her words settles over us like a heavy fog, pressing against our chests, stealing the air.

Neither of us move. Neither of us speak.

We just sit, absorbing the weight of it all. The weight of that choice.

Haunted by hindsight.

It drapes over us both like a shroud.

Finally, she speaks. Her voice is quiet, but firm. *"I'm not going to do it."*

I look toward the darkness. "Do what?"

"I'm not going to forgive myself. That's why you're here, right? To help me feel better about my fucked-up choice."

I don't say anything.

I just lower my head.

Heartbroken for the pain she puts herself through. Like it's penance for a forgiveness that will never come.

I can feel her eyes on me from somewhere in the shadows, waiting for me to contradict her. To tell her she's wrong.

I don't.

"I'm not going to do it," she repeats. *"It's unforgivable. You know what happened. You know how they were. You know the environment they created. The screaming matches. The doors slamming. The tension in the air."*

She pauses. Her voice sharpens. *"Multiple times a week."*

I exhale slowly, steadying myself. "Yeah, I know. And I also know how you torture yourself for it. I know how you blame yourself."

She laughs, but it's hollow.

"I should *blame myself."*

Her voice is frail now, like it's barely holding itself together beneath her shame.

"I sent my son to be with a volatile man. Who was in a relationship with a volatile woman. For 50 percent of his childhood. He ended up seeing the very things I tried to protect him from."

I hear her swallow hard.

"I failed him."

The words hit like a hammer, heavy and absolute.

"I had a chance to have my son more. To fight for him. To keep him safe. And I didn't do it. My job as his mother was to protect him, and I didn't do it."

Her breath is ragged.

"And I won't forgive myself for it."

I can't bear the silence that follows.

I don't know if she's still there or if she's slipped further into the darkness.

But she has it all wrong.

I wasn't expecting her to forgive herself.

I know she can't.

Because I haven't yet.

And I don't know if I ever will.

8.

Fire

"20s Me?"

I call to the shadows, searching for her in the darkness. I know she's still there.

She doesn't answer right away, but I can feel her. The energy shifts, like she's deciding whether or not to come back.

"There's more to your story."

I keep my voice steady, gentle. I don't want to push her. But she's so close now. So close to getting it all out.

Silence.

I wait.

I know she's exhausted. I know this has been more than she ever thought she could say.

"Can you share the last part? I know you're tired."

Still nothing.

But then, I hear her take a breath. It's shaky, uneven.

"Do you think she'll be mad?"

Her voice is small. Like she's bracing herself for something.

I don't have to ask who she means.

"Probably." I don't sugarcoat it. There's no point. "But do you really care?"

Silence stretches between us. She's done this dance before.

She's playing out the possible outcomes in her head, deciding whether this story is worth the consequences.

I can almost hear her mind racing, cycling through old patterns. The instinct to protect *her*—to shrink, to soften the truth, to make it easier for *her* to swallow—is still there.

It's still automatic.

But something is different this time.

I feel the shift before she even speaks.

Then—

"Fuck it."

Her voice is steady now.

Final.

The instinct is still there.

But so is the fight.

Walking

Six weeks after I finalized my divorce, my stepfather had prostate surgery. Early-stage prostate cancer. Routine procedure.

As part of his recovery, he had to take walks every couple of hours. I went to my mother's house to stay while he recovered. To walk with him multiple times a day. To make it easier on my mother.

She wanted me to help with the dogs. I told her no. I refused to help a puppy mill.

Within hours of my arrival, she had already stopped talking to me.

Some things don't ever change. No matter how old you get.

I stayed in the guest bedroom. My old bedroom. The one where it had happened.

I tried not to think about it. I just wanted to forget. It had been almost fifteen years. I thought I should be over it. But the reminders and flashbacks in that room told me I wasn't.

I needed to keep busy. To stay out of that room. Out of my head.

So, my stepfather and I walked.

And walked.

And walked.

He talked about a lot of things. How much he hated having so many dogs. How it embarrassed him sometimes. How much he just wanted to relax and not always have chores to do.

He talked about how hard it was when she would withhold love and attention from me and my sister. How hard it was when she did it to him.

He told me he had thought about leaving years before. That he didn't, because he didn't want to miss me and my sister.

It surprised me to learn he would miss me. I don't know why. It just didn't seem like him. At least not the version I remembered.

We talked about when my sister left. How strange it was not to have her in the house.

He opened up to me. Talked to me like I was an adult.
Not just his stepdaughter.

It was the most honest conversation we had ever had.

Eventually, we talked about what happened to me. What my *brother* did. What they allowed to happen.

When I first brought it up, we stood by a neighbor's farm. About a mile from my mother's house. My stepfather hung his head. He got quiet. He wouldn't look at me. His shoulders slumped.

He said he didn't know it had affected me. That they didn't know there was a problem.

It bothered me. To hear it said out loud. To hear him say, "We thought you were fine."

I knew my mask was good. I just didn't know it was *that* good.

I didn't know it was good enough to fool the people who were supposed to know me best. The ones who should have been looking for a problem.

I didn't expect my family to fall for it. To go on like nothing had happened. I didn't expect them to ignore me after what I had endured.

I had more language to put behind what I felt now. More than I had when I was eleven. Or twelve. Thirteen. Fourteen.

I was a parent now.

I could see their failure through an adult's lens. A parent's lens.

No matter which way I looked at it, what they did always looked like failure. It looked like selfishness. Like their comfort was worth more than my pain.

How could he look at me and say they *thought* I was fine?

Where was their protective nature? Why didn't they fight for me? Why didn't they fight to save me from my *brother*?

Parents are supposed to protect their children. Parents are supposed to fight.

So where was their fight? Where was their rage?

Was he lying? Trying to cover his own ass?

Or was it easier?

Easier to ignore me. To pretend had nothing happened. Forget the deadbolt on my bedroom door.

Did they avoid checking on me because they didn't *want* to know? Because they wanted to maintain the mask?

Or was I just not worth the effort?

I had to know. (And I did.) How much I meant to them. Or how little.

I asked my stepfather.

The look of shame deepened on his face. His eyes got sadder. He was thinking about what to say.

I watched his eyes dart around.

I wanted him to say it. I wanted him to say, *I should have protected you.*

I thought maybe this was the moment: He would say the obvious. He would say they *fucked up.*

Or whatever the Christian version of that was.

But he didn't.

He tried to change the subject. Tried to talk about a project my mother wanted him to do. He told me the doctor just needed to give him the green light to start doing more physical activity.

I brought the conversation back. I wouldn't let him hide from it.

"Why didn't you help me?"

He said they didn't know it was *that* bad. That they *would have* helped if they knew.

He asked me why I didn't ask for help.

My stomach dropped.

What the fuck?!

Was he actually serious? I had to *speak up* before they would know I needed help?

Are they fucking idiots?

A feeling rose from deep within. One I seldom entertained anymore.

Anger.

Anger always scared me. Nothing good ever came from it. At least not in my experience.

I wouldn't let myself feel it back then. I still don't now.

But it *washed* over me at that moment. I couldn't control it. Just for a second.

A fiery feeling.
Electric.
Coming from my core.

My jaw clenched. My hands squeezed into fists. My fingernails cut into my palms.

I felt the anger move through me. A righteous anger.

How dare *they blame* me *for* their *failures.*

Is that how they can sleep at night? Because they don't think they did anything wrong?

Have they had a clear conscience *this whole time?*

My mind swirled. I wanted to cuss him out. To hit him. To scream, *I didn't do anything wrong!*

Instead, I took a breath. Looked forward.

And reminded him—I *did* say something. Multiple times. When it all started. And no one believed me.

He shifted his step. Slowed down for a second.

He didn't deny it. Didn't tell me I was wrong. Didn't say anything.

He just kept walking.

I don't know why I thought he might do anything different. (But I did.)

He usually handled conflict like this: He would shut down.

Every time my mother was cruel to me. To my sister. To him.

He cowered. His spine dissolved.

And we were all on our own.

Every step forward was proof of what I had always known: He was weak. Weaker than me.

And it was then that I knew.

There would be no real reckoning. No real acknowledgment of what I endured. No real accountability for his failure. No real admission that I deserved better.

Only a man who was willing to feel ashamed—but not willing to feel responsible.

He could keep walking.

But I wouldn't let him take me with him.

The Candy Counter

When I was sixteen, my *brother* showed up at my work.

I worked as a lifeguard at the pool. I wanted to save people from drowning. The way that mother saved me years before.

It was sunny that day. Hot. The pool was already busy, and it wasn't even noon yet.

I sat near the entry. Near the bathrooms and changing rooms. A glass counter. Brightly colored bags of candy lining its shelves. Like at the movie theaters.

I bought a snack for my break. Talked to my manager about my schedule.

Out of the corner of my eye, I saw someone walking toward the entry. Something about him caught my attention. I didn't know what.

My stomach dropped.

I recognized him immediately.

Acne still covered his face. He looked just as mean. Like a rat ready to attack.

He didn't see me. He paid the entry fee and walked in.

I hid off to the side, next to the candy counter. Crouched down. Held my breath.

My manager looked confused. I mouthed the words, *I'm not here.*

She didn't understand. Her face contorted like she didn't know what to do.

He came to the counter. Asked for me.

I heard his voice say my name. "Megan."

My skin went cold. My heart raced. My breathing became shallow. Rapid. My hands started shaking.

My manager lied and said I wasn't there. I made myself as small as I could.

He said, "Okay," turned around, and left.

When he was gone, fully out of sight, I stood back up. My manager was worried. She asked if it was an ex-boyfriend.

My skin crawled.

Gross.

I told her he wasn't. Just a guy from when I was little. That he didn't like me. I didn't feel safe around him.

I didn't say anything else. I didn't have to.

He came back the next day.

I wasn't working.

My manager told him I was off for the week. That he'd need to talk to me somewhere else.

He didn't come back.

That was the last time I saw him in person. And, thankfully, he didn't see me.

On one of the walks with my stepfather, I asked how my *brother* knew where I worked.

I was living at my dad's house back then. My dad wouldn't have told him.

There could only be one way he would have known: My mother had talked to him. She told him where to find me.

My stepfather confirmed it on the walk.

I had known all along that must have been how he found me. That *she sent him.* I didn't want to believe it. I held on to a sliver of hope it wasn't true.

Hearing my stepfather say it felt like a stab to the chest. Searing-hot. Like from a fire poker. Another scar branded on my heart by my mother.

He said my *brother* showed up at my mother's house. One day. Out of the blue.

It was summer. Hot.

My stepfather said it was when my *brother* was sixteen. No longer at the group home. But my stepfather couldn't remember where he was staying.

My mother talked to him in the side yard outside of the house. For a while.

My stepfather said he stayed for part of their conversation. But not all.

Long enough to hear her betray me. But not long enough to stick up for me. Not long enough to protect me.

He wanted to get his chores done.

My mother was mad at me for moving to my dad's.

When my *brother* asked about me, my mother told him where I was living. Where I was working.

She didn't even hesitate.

Prison

The Christmas before my stepfather's surgery, my then-husband and I went to my mother's house.

These visits always felt forced. I attended solely out of obligation.

I never wanted to be there. I couldn't wait to leave.

He and I were at the lowest point in our marriage. I had already decided to leave. But I pretended. I didn't have the money to act yet.

We opened gifts. My mother took a picture of us by the Christmas tree. My ex, my son, and me.

Then she casually mentioned—she got a letter from my *brother*.

He was in prison.

For doing the same things to someone else that he did to me.

She asked if I wanted to read the letter, a devilishness to her voice. She knew what she was doing.

She got the letter from her office. I could see his handwriting on the outside of the envelope. His inmate number.

I felt dirty just looking at it. Why didn't she?

She dangled the letter in front of me. Like it was a prize.

I told her I didn't want to read it. I didn't care what he had to say. I was glad he was in prison. He belonged there.

And he was going to be there for 22.5 years.

I wondered if that felt like justice to the child he hurt. To the child's family.

I was glad he was being punished for what he did. I hoped prison was hard for him. I hoped he was scared at night. I hoped he had to hide from the other inmates. That he was beaten. And fucked with.

I wanted him to know fear. The kind he created for me.

I wanted him to feel relief when his cell door locked. Knowing the lock would keep the monsters out for the night. I hoped it was a deadbolt, even though I knew it was something stronger.

I wanted him to feel trapped by it, too. I wanted a piece of him to die every time he heard the lock. I wanted him to suffer.

I'm not proud of that fact. But it's the truth.

I asked my mother not to write him back.

She smirked.

She said that Jesus would turn the other cheek. So, that's what she was going to do.

She told me to do the same. Like I could just forget what he did to me. What she *let* him do.

I asked again. "Please don't write him back." I was begging.

I told her it would hurt me. I needed her to listen to me. To keep him away. To keep me safe.

She told me I was ridiculous. But ultimately, she said okay.

She said she wouldn't write him back. She promised.

On one of the walks with my stepfather after his surgery, I found out she had lied.

She wrote him back.

My stepfather said he didn't know what she wrote in her letter.

I didn't know if I believed him.

The Final Straw

I fumed on the inside.

She fucking lied to me.

My stepfather could tell I was upset. I couldn't hide it on my face.

He tried to make up reasons for her.

"It's hard to walk away from someone you see as your son. She didn't want to leave him with no one. He needed a reason to keep going."

I listened to all his excuses. Excuse. After excuse. After excuse.

I wanted to scream at my stepfather. To somehow force him to see the truth. She was still protecting a predator. And he was helping her do it.

At the same time, I wanted to give my stepfather the benefit of the doubt. I always did. He was more sympathetic than her. Like a wounded animal. Or an exhausted spouse, worn down by years of tiptoeing around her emotions. Of maintaining her mask.

I always felt conflicted about my stepfather. On the one hand, he had to deal with her, too. More than any of us. On the other hand, he was the one who installed the deadbolt. He was complicit in everything, and I still felt bad for him.

We walked back to the house. Each step moved me closer to what was coming.

I was going to face her.

I hated confronting her. I always did. It felt hard. Icky. Like I was a little kid again. Like she was larger than life. Looming over me.

But I couldn't let this stand. I couldn't let her get away with it.

When we got home, I confronted her about writing him back.

She lied to my face.

She told me she didn't do it. That she respected my wishes. That she kept her promise.

She looked me in the eyes when she said it.

I told her I knew she was lying. That my stepfather had told me the truth.

She glared at him. He shifted in his seat. He knew he was in trouble.

She was quiet for a second. Pondering her next move.

I knew what she did and I had a witness, so she had only one card left to play.

She admitted it.

"Okay, so I did. So what?"

I stared at her in disbelief.

"What do you mean, 'So what?'?!"

I shouted at her. Told her she was a terrible mother.

She told me I was a terrible daughter.

She was mad that I didn't help with the dogs.

Like breaking her promise meant nothing. Like hurting me meant nothing.

Everything was always going to be about what I could do for her. How her life could be easier. How I was only worth anything when I was doing something to help her.

I was never worth protection. Or the truth.

I packed up my stuff immediately and drove the two hours home.

I didn't speak to her after that.

Two weeks later, I got a DM from a family friend.

They had gone to dinner with my mother and stepfather. My mother was talking about me. Said I was mad for no reason. Downplayed it all. Wanted to be the victim.

But she also let something slip.

"If Megan's mad about the letter, imagine how she'd feel about the picture."

The family friend said she kinda laughed when she said it.

My mother sent my *brother* a picture when she wrote him back.

It was the picture from Christmas.

By the tree.

The one of me.

My ex-husband.

And my son.

She gave him a picture of my son. She wanted him to see my life. Like he was family.

I imagined him opening the letter. The picture falling into his lap. His hands holding it. His eyes staring. Analyzing.

Did he take in how my body had changed? Did he search for pain in my eyes? The pain *he* caused?

Did he hang the picture on his wall? To remind himself of what he did to me? Like a trophy? Did he pretend I was his family?

Or did he fix his gaze on my son?

The questions overwhelmed me. The fear was palpable.

She put my life in his hands again. And she laughed about it.

I didn't question the story. I didn't wonder if the family friend was telling the truth. I knew they were.

I knew my mother would lie if asked about it.

I couldn't trust her. Not what she said. Not what she did.

I didn't even have to think about it. I knew I was done the second I read that DM.

Fuck her. Fuck my mother.

It felt wrong to call her *my mother*. Mothers don't do what she did.

I decided right then not to call her *my mother* anymore.

I would call her by her first name. The most ironic of all first names. One I couldn't make up if I tried.

Joy.

- -

20s Me stops talking. But the rage in her voice lingers. So does the exhaustion.

She's been through so much. And she's so tired.

I want to reassure her.

"You made the right choice. Going no-contact with her. You know that, right?"

"I know."

"I still haven't spoken to her. Fifteen years later. Not once."

"I know."

20s Me stays quiet. But I know she's still here.

"We don't need her, 20s Me. We never have."

"I know."

"We have Robynn. She believes us. She knows the truth now. She is our family."

"Yeah."

I feel the loneliness radiating from her.
Like waves coming off hot pavement.
Tangible. Almost visible. Even from the shadows.
I know how hard this is for her.
She's done almost everything alone.
Carried everything alone.

"Joy's going to lie and say it's not true. She's going to say I made it up. Or that I'm being 'dramatic.'"

"She probably will. But we expect that. She'll just be proving she's exactly who we think she is: a bully and a coward."

Silence.

"What if Robynn believes her? What if we lose the only family we have?"

"We won't. Robynn doesn't trust her either. We're not alone anymore."

I wait. Letting it sit between us. Letting her feel the weight of it.

Then I add, "It doesn't matter what she thinks.
It's not her story to tell.
You didn't tell it for her.
You told it for you. And me."

I smile.

"Remember what we say when we hear her voice in our head? Telling us we're not good enough? Or too much?"

"Yeah, I remember."

"Then say it with your full fucking chest. Like you could scream it in her face."

I hear 20s Me sigh. A sharp inhale. Like she's gathering the strength inside herself.

I don't know if she'll do it. If she'll feel brave enough.

I want her to say it so badly. To feel the words come from her bones. Not just her mouth.

The silence stretches.

But then I hear it.

Loud. Unmistakable.

"Fuck her."

I smile.

That's my girl.

9.

The Steadiest Thing

"30s Me?"

I know this version of myself well. She doesn't scare me the way the others do. She holds the beauty of my life. I visit her frequently.

"Yeah?"

She steps forward, emerging from the shadows and into the light of my awareness.

She looks…happy. Really happy.

Her pixie cut is sharp, bold—the post-divorce change. New hair. New life.

So cliché. So necessary.

Her face brightens as she moves closer, her eyes shimmering with life. A slow smile spreads across her face. Big. Bright. Teeth showing.

She knows why I'm here.

"I was hoping we could talk about Jason."

Her whole body responds, leaning forward, drawn in by his name alone. It's like she can't help it. Like just the thought of him is enough to warm her from the inside out.

She grins wider, practically glowing. Her happiness is contagious.

"Anything in particular you want to know, or are we just cruising down memory lane?"

Her voice is lighter than 20s Me's. It has an ease to it. A playfulness. Like someone who finally knows joy.

I can already feel myself smiling back. I try to hold it in, but I don't think I can.

"Whatever you want to share about him is perfect."

Her smirk turns mischievous. She tilts her head slightly, considering.

Then, without hesitation, she plops down. Comfortable. Like she owns the place. Like she belongs here.

And she does.

She leans back on her hands, stretching her legs out in front of her, rolling her ankles absentmindedly as if settling into a familiar story.

Her smile shifts again, smaller now, more knowing.

"Let me start by telling you how I met him. How a single click of the mouse changed my life *forever.*"

Her voice hums with nostalgia, anticipation. She's ready to tell me everything.

And I'm ready to listen.

Match

I had been divorced for eighteen months.

I wasn't interested in dating. I refused to get into anything long-term.

I felt comfortable alone. Safe alone.

I didn't have the energy to learn someone else's idiosyncrasies. The energy to be on high alert with someone new. I was already on high alert all the time.

Being single was easier. I only had to look out for myself, my son, and Bailey.

Katherine encouraged me to try online dating. Persistently.

After a little too much sangria, we sat down and made my profile. We published it before I could change my mind.

It was the early days of online dating, when it was still embarrassing to tell people you met that way.

I didn't like the gooey, romantic vibes in the eHarmony commercials, so I bought a six-month membership to Match.com instead.

The first night, people started messaging me—men asking to take me to dinner, to tell me about their adventures.

My profile had pictures from a paleontology dig I had gone on that summer. I thought it made me seem interesting.

I also posted pictures from Bonnaroo—the trip I took with Katherine and my best friend, Amanda.

I must've picked the right pictures.

Within an hour, my inbox filled with stories from potential matches. Someone had gone to Peru. Someone else enjoyed surfing. One guy collected bugs.

It all felt normal.

I scrolled through their pictures, wondering what other women looked for when they did the same. What did they see?

Were they looking at their muscles? At what they did for a living? Their hobbies?

I didn't see them that way. I wondered which one of them would abuse their partners. Which one would call me stupid.

I couldn't do it.

After Katherine left, I made my profile invisible and forgot about it.

But she didn't stop asking me. She really wanted me to see that not everybody was like my ex-husband.

I wasn't willing to take that chance.

Months passed. I never opened the app. I wasn't interested.

Then, I got an email from Match. They were reaching out to see if I wanted to extend my membership.

I only had one month left.

I logged in, planning to cancel. When I opened the app, the screen showed my suggested matches.

The first was a cute guy with brown hair and a beard. He had beautiful eyes. Hazel.

I clicked on his profile and saw that he loved music. Went to live shows.

In some pictures, he had a beard. In others, he didn't.

I wondered which he had now.

At the bottom of his profile, there was a button: *Click to wink at Jason.*

I didn't know why, but I clicked it.

A single click of the mouse. One that would notify him I saw something I liked.

I got so anxious about *winking* at him that I closed the app without canceling my subscription.

That night, I got an email. From him.

The message was long, well-written, and thoughtful. It was clear he had spent time looking at my profile, thinking about the questions he wanted to ask me.

I wrote him back. My hands shook with every tap on the keyboard.

What am I doing? Why am I talking to him?

The next morning, I had another email from him. Just as long. Just as thoughtful.

This became our routine.

For weeks, we emailed daily. Sometimes multiple times a day. Every single time, my stomach knotted together—both terrified and exhilarated.

After two weeks, he asked if we could get together for dinner.

I told him I couldn't. That I had my son and would be out of town at a concert that weekend.

He asked about the following weekend.

I didn't have my son then. My ex-husband was taking him on a trip.

Jason asked to meet me at a new brewery that had just opened.

He gave me his number in case plans changed.

I almost canceled a thousand times.

I was terrified.

It's embarrassing to admit, but I had Katherine call him first. I was muted on the line. She pretended to be looking for someone else.

I needed to hear his voice. I needed to hear it to know I was safe. To know *he* was safe.

He sounded kind.

Not rude when Katherine said she was looking for a friend. He simply said she had the wrong number. Then, before hanging up, he added, "I hope you find who you're looking for."

That extra step. That tiny sentence.

It told me everything I needed to know.

I decided to meet him at the brewery.

The Shoe Master General

He waited outside for me. He wore an unbuttoned blue and white plaid shirt, the sleeves rolled slightly. Underneath it, a T-shirt with the Union Jack stretched across his chest.

He was tall. Handsome. Looked exactly like his pictures. He had a beard in real life.

I liked it.

We walked into the bar area, sat down, and ordered our beers.

The conversation started effortlessly, like we had known each other for years. No awkward pauses. No uncomfortable silences.

He told me about his family, his job, and his first marriage. No kids.

I listened to every word. Time had stopped, like he and I were the only ones in the bar.

I had plans to meet some friends after the date. Katherine wanted to know everything. About an hour in, I slipped into the bathroom, called her, and told her I wasn't coming.

We sat there for hours, talking. Laughing. Everything was just so easy.

He listened to me. Asked questions to understand me more. It felt strange—like I was being interviewed for a job by a friend.

I was nervous the entire time. Afraid to say the wrong thing. To mess up. But I didn't let him know that.

I wanted him to think I was charming, funny, and smart.

As we talked at the bar, the guy sitting next to me got progressively drunker. And drunker. And drunker.

He kept trying to get my attention.

Jason was annoyed but patient. He wasn't rude or mean.

The drunk guy introduced himself as the Shoe Master General. He claimed to own a lot of shoes. Said he liked mine. Gold Sperry's.

I smiled, nodded, and turned my attention back to Jason. We giggled about my drunk neighbor. Our first inside joke.

After a while, we got up from the bar and walked outside, hoping for fewer interruptions.

That plan failed immediately.

I spotted a dog on the patio. I made my way toward it without hesitation. Jason was just as excited as I was.

My heart skipped a beat.

The couple with the dog started talking to me. Then, they started talking to Jason.

I expected him to get frustrated—another disruption on our first date.

But he didn't. He just rolled with it.

We stood and talked with them for a while. They were nice. Funny—they couldn't believe we had just met.

They thought we had been together for years. They had immediately noticed the comfort between us.

They were heading to another brewery nearby. Said they didn't want to interrupt our date but asked if we wanted to join them.

Jason looked at me, waiting for my cue. I nodded.

He told them we'd meet them there.

I got into Jason's car—a gray Volkswagen Jetta. I laughed. I drove the exact same car. Mine was red.

We arrived at the second brewery, only to find a wedding reception in full swing. Closed to the public.

The couple we met decided to call it a night. They didn't want to take up any more of our first date.

I wasn't deterred. I believed I could talk my way into the reception.

I was right.

I was nailing this whole being charming thing.

We had one drink outside. With the bride.

Then we left.

Jason asked if I wanted to go somewhere else or if I wanted to go back to my car.

I chose somewhere else.

I didn't know why. I felt a push-pull happening inside me. Part of me wanted to hide from Jason. To keep myself safe.

The other part already knew I was safe. It knew I was safe with him.

We stayed at the third bar until it closed.

He drove me back to my car. No pressure. No expectations. No first-date kiss.

But at the last bar, he placed his hand on my knee. His quiet way of telling me he was enjoying our date.

When he touched me, I expected my body to jump. My muscles to tighten. I expected to feel the fear.

I did jump. My muscles did tighten.

But the fear never came.

Only the butterflies.

Safety

I drove home after the date, but I couldn't sleep. I felt high. And nervous.

I couldn't put my finger on what it was about him that made me feel safe. I didn't understand it.

I didn't trust anyone. Not really. But for some reason, I wanted to trust him.

I replayed the night over and over, searching for any red flags. Anything to make my feelings not real. I couldn't find any.

I even tried to create red flags in my mind. But I couldn't do it.

At every turn, Jason showed me he was a good person.

At every turn, he showed me he was safe.

At every turn, he showed me he was not like the people who had hurt me.

I kept my armor up around him. But I had a feeling that I didn't have to.

From the first email he wrote, to the first time I heard his voice, to our first date—he always made me feel safe.

I apologized for everything. The littlest things. Conditioning that hadn't gone away.

Jason never got mad at me for apologizing. He would gently remind me, "You don't have to apologize for that." Or, "You didn't do anything wrong."

He confused me. Not in a bad way. I just didn't know what to do with someone who was nice.

He wore his kindness on his sleeve. He was genuine and sincere. Proud to be a good guy.

I wondered if it was a mask. *Is he hiding something?* But I never found anything that said he was.

Everything about him seemed and felt true.

Our first date lasted seven hours. Enough time for me to know I wanted to see him again. But not enough time to let go of any of my armor.

I sat in my bed that night running it all through my head. Trying to make it make sense.

When I was with him, everything felt easier. More stable.

Like the world wasn't tilted on its axis as much. Like I wasn't tilted as much.

I expected dread. But I felt none.

And that scared the fuck out of me.

But not enough to run from him.

Hope

The day after our first date, I spent time working on a paper for college. My second undergraduate degree. Desperate for a break.

He texted me that morning to say he had a great time the night before. He asked what I had planned for the day.

I told him I planned to take a walk. That I needed to get away from writing for a bit.

I asked if he wanted to meet me. I didn't expect him to say yes. It was last minute, after all.

But he did.

He showed up at the park on time. We walked and talked. It was just as easy as the night before.

Turns out, it wasn't the beer. He genuinely found me interesting.

We walked for a while. He drove me to my car. He kissed me on the cheek.

More butterflies.

We made plans to meet up during the week. After my class.

I was still waiting for the red flags. Waiting for the catch. Waiting for the other shoe to drop. But they never came.

That Wednesday night, we met at a bar. A different brewery from our first date. We talked and talked and talked. Closed the bar down.

After midnight, ours were the only cars left in the parking lot, other than the service staff.

He walked me to my car. Held my hand. Leaned in and kissed me.

Sparks shot through me.

I didn't know kisses could feel electric.

It started to rain.

We quickly planned another date for later in the week. He would take me to a baseball game. A playoff game. He was impressed that I could keep score.

We went our separate ways.

His text came through when I got back to my apartment.

If it wasn't for the rain, I'd still be kissing you in that parking lot.

My heart felt like it might explode out of my chest. And for the first time in a long time, I took a whole breath. I filled my lungs. All the way. And exhaled deeply.

That exhale held every unspoken fear. It held my doubts about being lovable. About being enough. Being too much.

And for just a moment, I let them go.

With that one breath, I created space. Space for Jason. For a truth that contradicted everything I had known. For a new kind of air to breathe.

Mary Oliver once asked, "Are you breathing just a little and calling it a life?"

For the first time, I understood exactly what she meant.

I was weeks away from turning thirty,
and for the first time in my life,
I was breathing fully.

Maybe there was hope for me after all. And maybe hope went by the name Jason.

Scrapbooks

I knew in that moment, in the brewery parking lot. When he kissed me in the rain. Sparks erupting.

I knew I was falling for him.

It felt quick. It was quick. It made me think this might be a trap. Like I needed to keep one eye open and on him at all times.

We went to the baseball game that weekend. It was fun. We skipped through the stadium—my idea. Forty-five thousand people around. He didn't care. He skipped his heart out.

I texted Robynn a picture of us together. She liked his teeth. I liked everything about him.

His long arms. The light speckles of white in his beard. The way his eyes lit up when he made me laugh. The way he smelled.

He didn't wear cologne. He smelled like deodorant and body wash. Clean.

I wondered what he liked about me. If he could see what bubbled beneath the surface: Shame.

I felt dirty. I came with baggage. Childhood abuse. Intimate partner violence.

Could he handle it?

Could he handle me?

When I was with him, I didn't judge my past. But when I was alone, my mind constantly told me he was too good for me. That I was too much for him. That he deserved someone who didn't carry so much bullshit. So much pain.

I didn't know how to earn his love. What did I need to do to deserve it?

He came from a completely different world. He had a close-knit family that relished group activities. He called his brothers. He never wondered if he was loved.

His mom made scrapbooks. When he was in high school, Casey cut out every newspaper article that mentioned his name. He played basketball. So there were a lot of articles. She wanted him to feel her pride.

He told me what it felt like to lose her. She died from a brain aneurysm years before I met him. I liked when he told stories about her.

She was a force—I could tell. A woman who deeply loved her children. A mother who wanted her boys to grow up to be good men. Incredible. Someone I would have loved to meet.

I met his family for the first time at Thanksgiving. They were Italian, so they were loud and there were a lot of them.

His dad had a twin brother. Identical. I couldn't tell them apart.

The house was full of people. Warm and inviting.

Jason's step mom, Becky, instantly made me feel welcome. She was kind and hugged me. She told me she could see how happy Jason was. She thanked me for being the reason.

I wanted to impress them. To make him proud to introduce me to them.

But I also felt strange. Like I was an anthropologist studying how they lived. There wasn't an ounce of dysfunction to be found.

No tension. No anger. No unease.

Nothing I was used to.

I wondered if they were studying me, too.

I hadn't told Jason anything about my past. Not really.

The pain. The suffering. My desperate need for safety. I kept it all shoved down. My mask held tightly in place.

But could they see it? Could Jason?

When the evening ended, would his family tell him the obvious truth? That he could do better? That he could find someone who wasn't so fucked up?

They seemed like the kind of family that would protect one another. Would Jason need to be protected from me?

Am I the red flag?

My mind swirled.

I wanted to belong. But love in Jason's world spoke a different language.

And I wasn't sure if I'd ever be fluent.

Strong

It always sounded crazy when I told people, but Jason and I didn't fight.

Ever.

We talked about everything. It never got to that point. No raised voices. No trying to prove the other wrong. We always assumed best intentions.

I didn't have to struggle to be heard. Or seen. He loved me however I could show up. However much I would let him see me.

I always worried he'd leave. That he would wake up and realize I wasn't worth the effort. That he would realize he was too good for me. But he never did.

He just showed up. Over and over and over again. He kept proving to be exactly who I thought he was.

I kept myself hidden. Only telling parts of my story. Just enough so he wouldn't ask questions. Just enough so he wouldn't wonder where my parents were.

Before I introduced him to my son, we went to dinner with my ex-husband.

I didn't want to go. I didn't want to subject Jason to him. But I also knew it was the right thing to do. I knew my son deserved that.

Jason sat through dinner. He tolerated my ex-husband being extra whiny because his wife refused to join us. They had been married for a few months and fought regularly. My ex-husband already seemed miserable.

Karma has a twisted sense of humor.

After dinner, Jason and I laughed about it. Grateful it wasn't us.

We knew we were building something strong. Something better. And we were both proud of it.

I didn't always know how to feel safe in the space I created for him.

Or the space he created for me.

But we were building something real. And I never had to wonder if Jason knew it, too.

He made sure I always knew.

Promises

I felt paralyzed by the fear of losing him. Like maybe the pain wasn't going to come from him, from abuse. But from his loss. And I wouldn't be able to bear it.

One time, he went to work. He didn't text me when he got there like normal. He went straight into meetings.

I waited for his text. It never came. I started to panic.

I pictured him lying on the roadside. Mangled and bloody.

I tried to call his phone. It went straight to voicemail.

The panic intensified. I started hyperventilating. Crying.

I wondered if I should call the hospitals. *Would they even tell me anything since we aren't married?* I thought about calling the police to check for accidents along his route.

The fear consumed every single logical thought I had. I operated entirely out of panic.

This went on for a couple of hours. I called again. Left another voicemail.

This time, I couldn't hide the fear. I sobbed as I spoke.

He called me a half hour later. Apologized profusely for scaring me.

He never made me feel bad about it. Never made me feel guilty. But he had every right to.

My reaction wasn't rational. It wasn't logical.

And he loved me anyway.

He said he never wanted me to be scared like that. Promised to always text when he got to work. And when he left. That way I would always know when to expect him.

He saw my fear and didn't blame me for it. He didn't get mad. He worked with it.

He worked with me.

This was just one of thousands of ways he held me.

One of thousands of ways he made me feel safe.

One of thousands of ways he made space for me.

One of thousands of ways he loved me out loud.

And he never broke his promise.

Anchor

Jason had this way of reading me. Of picking up on the subtle changes in my behavior. He could tell when I was starting to panic.

But he never panicked. He stayed calm. He reminded me to breathe. He held me when I needed him to. And stayed back when I didn't.

It was like I was built to be held by him.

He stood 6 foot 4. My forehead barely reached the middle of his chest. When he hugged me, he wrapped his arms around me. Rested his head on mine. It was his way of drawing me in closer. When I got lost in my mind, he brought me back into my body. Back into the moment.

I could hear his heartbeat. The most soothing sound I knew. It reminded me to breathe fully. To let him love me. Even when I didn't feel worthy of it.

Every morning, he woke up early. Got ready for work. Then climbed back into bed.

He was always there before my first alarm went off. My second alarm, set for fifteen minutes later, was a backup.

During that time, I would sleepily roll over. Lay my head on his chest. And he would wrap his arms around me.

His heartbeat became my wake-up call. A rhythm pulling me back to the present moment. Inviting me into a new day.

Ba-dum.

Ba-dum.

Ba-dum.

His heartbeat was the steadiest thing I had ever known.

Patience

I revealed my past in pieces.

I didn't want to give it all away, only for him to run. Not that I would have blamed him.

But that wasn't Jason.

Every awful truth. Every story. He held space for me to share. Never pushed me to speak before I was ready.

I had never known someone so patient. He waited over ten years to hear my full story. Over a decade for me to feel fully safe.

I waited, because reliving it was hard and made me feel so unworthy. Messy. Damaged.

He never saw me that way. He never has.

He loved me for me. Even when I didn't know what that meant. Even when I was still trying to figure it out.

He let me show up exactly as I was. Messy hair. Sweatpants. Cursing like a sailor.

He never made excuses for me. Never told me to be quieter. To shrink.

He was never embarrassed to be with me.

The opposite, actually.

He was proud. When I was his girlfriend. When I was his fiancée. When I was his wife.

He told me he loved me all the time. And every time, I knew he meant it.

I could always be certain of that.

Jason's love was one of the most precious gifts I had ever received. I used to hold it like it was fragile. Like I could stumble and break it in an instant.

But it wasn't fragile at all. It was the most solid thing I knew.

I knew so many relationships that would never reach where we were now. A space of absolute trust.

I couldn't always wrap my head around it. At times, it still seemed hard to believe. Like I was waiting for the universe's pendulum to swing the other way.

Even when I felt scared, I loved him fully. I loved him out loud. He deserved that.

He showed me a truth I should have already known.

That love wasn't supposed to be a battle. That I never had to earn it.

That I didn't have to understand it fully to accept it.

That no matter how many times my mind tried to convince me otherwise, his love was mine.

And it always would be.

30s Me literally swoons. Tears trail down her cheeks.

"He's going to hate this, you know."

I look at her. Our eyes lock.

"He's going to hate being put on a pedestal."

I smile. "I know."

We both roll our eyes and laugh.

He's predictable. But in the best kind of way.

30s Me straightens, wiping her cheeks with the sleeve of her sweater. Her expression shifts. The dreamy nostalgia remains, but something deeper settles in too. Something reverent.

"Do you ever stop and realize what he's given you?"

She scans my face, searching for truth.

I know what she's asking.

She's not talking about gestures. Not the kisses in the rain or the way he always texts when he gets to work. Not the way he wraps me up in his arms before my alarm goes off.

She's asking if I see the foundation beneath it all.

I nod, slowly. Because I do.

Jason gives me safety, but not just the kind that protects.
He gives me safety that allows me to exist fully.
Safety that doesn't require armor.
Safety that sees every piece of me and stays.

He shows me what it means to be loved without condition.
Not in the way people say they love you—
but in the way they prove it, day after day.

The kind of love I never believed in.
Until him.

"Is it easier to let him love you now?"

Her voice softens. She knows the weight of her question. She knows it holds everything.

I take a breath. I owe her honesty.

"Most days, yes. Some days, no. Sometimes I let the monster in my mind win. I get scared. I worry he feels trapped. Stuck, married to a crazy person. That he's too nice to say anything."

30s Me nods, her lips pressing together. She looks away for a moment, staring at something unseen.

"I still can't believe he never left."

She whispers it like a secret. Like a thought that still doesn't feel real to her.

"I waited for him to leave. Every single day. I thought—no, I knew—it was inevitable. That one day, he'd wake up and see me the way I saw myself. And he'd walk away. Not because he was cruel. But because I was never supposed to be the kind of person who got to keep someone like him."

She laughs, shaking her head at herself.

"I wasted so much time being scared."

"You did." I say it gently.

"Did you ever stop waiting?"

I tilt my head, considering.

"Not all at once."

She watches me carefully.

"I stopped piece by piece.
Every time he stayed.
Every time he kept his word.
Every time he told me he loved me
without asking for anything in return.
I didn't just *decide* to believe him.
I learned how to."

30s Me exhales. Not quite relief. Not quite regret. Something in between.

"I wish I had let myself fully feel it sooner."

"Me too."

She nods, sitting with that for a long moment.

The silence doesn't feel heavy. It softens into something like acceptance.

She takes another deep breath.

"I thought my fear would always win."

She looks at me now, and I see it—the part of her that fought so hard to believe in his love. The part of her that never stopped trying.

"But his love outlasted it."

Her voice is steady. She knows she's right.

Love stayed.
Love endured.
Love won.

And maybe that was the truth all along.

10.

Three Wise Women

30s Me doesn't step forward. She doesn't need to. She's still here.

She exhales, stretching her legs in front of her, flexing her feet. A quiet, familiar movement. A grounding movement.

Her head tilts slightly, eyes soft.

"You good?"

She knows something's off. She can sense it.

"Yeah, I just keep thinking about the monster of the mind."

Her expression shifts, just slightly. I catch it: a flicker of something—recognition, maybe.

She exhales through her nose.

"What about it?"

"Can you tell me why it scares you so much?"

She doesn't answer right away. She's thinking.

Finally, she speaks.

"For years, I thought I had to fight it alone," she says. *"That no one else could see it. No one else could hear it whispering all the ways I wasn't enough.*

"But that wasn't true, was it?"

I shake my head.

"Women have been battling the monster of doubt for centuries. Long before we even knew what it was."

"Yeah, but they didn't have to do it alone." Her voice softens, but there's a quiet urgency to it.

"They sat in circles. They held each other.
They stitched their stories into quilts and whispered their grief
into each other's hair.
They passed wisdom down like heirlooms. They reminded each other how
to keep going."

"You didn't do it alone either, 30s Me."

She glances at me.

Her voice is barely above a whisper. *"It felt like I did."*

I nod. I understand. Because I remember.

"There were women there to hold you. To love you. To support you."

She's quiet for a moment, letting it settle. Letting herself see it.

Then, something shifts. A slow smile creeps in. A different kind of recognition.

"Yeah," she says, nodding now. *"We were part of that, too. It just looked a little different."*

She leans back on her hands. Her smile turns knowing.

"There were three women who helped me face my monster." She pauses, like she's pulling their names from the warmth of memory.

"Brittni. Amanda. Brandi. They were my hands to hold. My breath when I couldn't catch my own. My proof that I didn't have to carry everything alone."

Her smile lingers. This time, it's gratitude.

"I thought I was fighting alone."

She exhales. Blinks. Sits up a little straighter. *"But I wasn't, was I?"*

"No," I say.

She nods, satisfied. Then tilts her head at me, playful now.

I smile back.

"Tell me about them. Starting with the one who taught us how to breathe?"

Her eyes light up instantly.

She knows exactly who I mean.

Brittni

When it happened, I froze.

At thirteen, my son stood at my bedroom door complaining. I don't remember what he was complaining about—just that it was unfair.

Then I heard it.

The voice of my ex-husband.

So clear. Real. Angry. Yelling on the other side of the door.

The past hit me like lockjaw, but in every joint in my body. I couldn't move even if I wanted to. My muscles tensed. My toes curled into the carpet. My breath went shallow. My heart raced.

I couldn't tell who was talking to me. I couldn't tell if it was my son or my ex-husband.

A feeling of fear, disgust, and sickness moved through me.

Not because I believed my son would act like my ex-husband.

But because, in that moment, my mind couldn't tell the difference.

And just like that—as fast as it happened, it ended.

I was back in my closet. Confused. Shaken. My heart still racing. My breath still too fast.

I knew I couldn't mother my son like that.

I knew I couldn't live like that.

Afraid. Wondering if it was going to happen again.

Or more often.

It was the first time I'd had an auditory flashback so crystal clear it felt like it was happening in real time.

I was used to flashbacks—images or thoughts that shot into my mind, then right out. Like an unwelcome guest. But this was different. There wasn't a memory, at least not more than what I heard outside the door.

Just his voice.

I spent the rest of the night in rabbit hole after rabbit hole on the Internet.

Am I losing my mind?

Do I need to get checked in somewhere?

The next morning, I made an appointment with a therapist.

I found her on the Psychology Today website.

I can't really tell you what drew me to her, but there was something

She was new to the practice, so I was able to get in quickly.

I felt nervous for my first session. I had barely told Jason what I'd experienced—how was I supposed to tell a complete stranger?

But my therapist, Brittni, masterfully put me at ease.

She worked with troubled kids before going into private practice. We connected over that.

She loved the kiddos who had lived hard lives. Just like I did.

That made it easier to talk to her.

In the early sessions, I gave her broad strokes.

Childhood sexual abuse. Intimate partner violence. Depression. Anxiety.

Enough to let her know I was complicated.

She figured it out pretty quickly.

She added C-PTSD to my list of challenges.

It explained a lot.

Why I struggled to trust people. Why I would leave my body, disappearing completely. Why I was constantly on alert. Why I was scared to be seen.

Bit by bit, she cut through the fog. Asking me questions to push my thinking. Challenging my limiting beliefs. Reframing things in a more empowering way. Helping me meet myself with more grace.

I treated therapy like school.

Brittni gave me homework every week, and I did it. Relentlessly.

I wanted to be a good student. To get therapy gold stars. To make her proud.

I relied on her validation. She knew my whole story and still told me I was a good person.

She also gave me ways to see it for myself.

She pointed out my impact in the lives of others.

Wife. Mother. Sister. Teacher. Friend.

"That's a lot of impact."

She was a mirror, showing me who I was—because I had forgotten.

She showed me my deep compassion. That my empathy was a strength. That I was more self-aware than I gave myself credit for.

Brittni taught me strategies for how to sit with compliments and not squirm. To set boundaries. To let go of control. To trust myself. She helped me see that my perspective wasn't wrong.

But it was also only one piece of a much larger puzzle.

She reminded me there are many ways to look at the same thing. Some that make me feel worse. Some that make me feel better.

But ultimately, I get to decide.

She called me out on my bullshit.

When I was cruel to myself for no reason. When I didn't make space for self-compassion.

She would tell me how she saw me.

I was strong. I was self-aware. Smart. Kind. Empathetic. Funny. I loved people deeply. I accepted people as they were. I was authentic. I was a good person.

I didn't let my traumas make me hard.

I liked how she saw me.

But I felt like I tricked her somehow.

Like if she only knew a little more, she'd realize I sucked.

But damn, that woman is patient.

Like when I talked about work.

Deep in burnout, I ached to feel something different.

When Brittni brought up leaving teaching, I resisted immediately.

I felt selfish. Guilty. I felt like choosing myself over the students meant I was failing—not just as a teacher, but as a person.

It gave me an immediate ick.

I wasn't going to do that.

My homework after that session was to draw it out. Whatever that meant—abstract or concrete—she wanted me to draw my life beyond teaching.

She wanted me to pay attention to how that prospect felt in my body.

So, I did.

And as I drew, I felt it.

Excitement for a life that was just a dream.

Just colors on a page.

But it felt big. Expansive. Radiating from my heart space.

It felt like freedom.

A desire to be in charge of me.

I stared at the life I had drawn.

A kaleidoscope.

A life full of opportunities.

And I heard it.

A small voice from within.

Not the voice of my inner critic. It was my inner knowing.

It's okay to want big things. You can have them. You just have to do the work.

I knew the voice was right. I felt it.

It felt peaceful.

I stayed in that feeling for as long as it lasted.

I was proud of myself.

The work was working.

The resistance remained, but now it had competition—a spark, a whisper of something more.

I got stuck in a loop—blaming myself, shaming myself, hating myself.

But the tiny voice would return. Not every time I reached for it. Not even often at first. But it was there.

This undercurrent of change.

Like the molecules inside me were rearranging themselves.

Nothing visible on the surface, but a growing felt sense in my body.

I didn't want to trust the voice. I worried it would set me up for pain. I worried that thinking I was a good person was tricking myself.

Every time I told Brittni something the voice told me, I got a therapy gold star. It was hard to deny the power of the voice when Brittni celebrated it right in front of me.

At times, the voice made me feel worse. Like something was wrong with me. Why couldn't I just believe what it said?

I felt like a failure.

The voice would tell me, *Trust the process.*

So I kept going.

Even when I felt like a failure. Even when sitting in that space felt unbearable.

I wanted to leave it. To get out of the ick.

The longer I sat there, the more I wondered if the voice was bullshit.

But then, I started to see changes in my life.

At first, they weren't visible to others. But they were noticeable to me.

Moments when I would normally berate myself, and I didn't.
Moments when I would try to control everything, and I let go.

Moments when I could recognize what was in my control and what wasn't.

Moments when I could analyze my actions from a higher perspective.

These moments didn't feel small.

They got my attention. I noticed every single one of them.

It's how I knew it was working. I was moving forward.

Eventually, people noticed the changes on the outside.

First Jason. Then Brittni. Then my best friend, Amanda.

The people closest to me saw it.

They said something.

And in those moments, I knew I could trust the voice.

When I could see it and feel it within. When others could see it on the outside.

It created momentum. Like a snowball rolling down a hill.

I just wanted to do more healing. More work. See more changes. Feel more differences. I wanted to let the voice within me grow louder.

I felt energized.

Both by the external recognition and the internal changes.

I had been underwater for a long time. And I finally got my first sips of air.

It was relief.

I always worried that the tide would pull me back under. That I would get a hint of what the air tasted like only to have it ripped away.

But I fought for it anyway.

The way a drowning person fights to find the surface.

I fought for healing.

Even though it scared the shit out of me. Even though I had no idea how to exist in a healed space.

But if I could just stay there long enough, keep my feet on the sand long enough, I knew I could keep breathing the air of relief.

I knew I would fight for that space for as long as it took.

The voice inside me kept telling me to keep going. To keep fighting. That it wasn't a race.

The air isn't going anywhere. I will get there when I get there. And the air will still taste just as fresh.

I wasn't just preparing to gasp for air. I was training my lungs to breathe differently.

And I wasn't doing it alone.

I had Brittni to guide me.

Therapy wasn't just about processing the past—it was about learning to live in the present.

Brittni helped me see I belonged in the space I created for myself.

And for the first time, I was breathing like I believed it.

Amanda

I met Amanda when our kids were still babies. My son was nine months old. Hers was six.

We met at a Gymboree class—socialization for babies and stay-at-home moms.

Amanda was funny. Outgoing. She seemed so secure in who she was. So powerful. I wanted to know her secret.

We started talking in class while the babies played. We went to lunch afterward. She was easy to be around. Fun to talk to.

We had a lot in common. She grew up not far from where I did—a college town. I used to go there all the time as a kid. We knew the same places.

She was open. Kind, but with a take-no-shit attitude. I loved that about her.

As the weeks and months passed, we started hanging out without our boys—going to dinner, getting drinks, taking long walks in the park.

We became increasingly present in each other's lives. She went to my son's birthday parties. I did the same for hers.

We made space for each other.

She was my first deep adult friendship.

She genuinely liked me. And I liked her.

I let myself trust her.

When things were getting bad with my ex-husband, I started opening up to her.

When my ex and I separated and I was living on my own in the apartment, she was one of my favorite people to spend time with.

She knew I needed her. That I needed a buoy in the storm.

We went to Bonnaroo together.

She didn't love being around Katherine, but she did it for me.

At Bonnaroo, Katherine did her own thing. Amanda and I did ours. We danced late into the night, laughing and feeling free.

Whenever we were together, it was always an adventure.

When Katherine and I stopped talking, Amanda was still there.

She listened when I told her about the fight Katherine and I had. How easy it was for me to cut her out of my life.

It's not a skill I'm proud of. Just a side effect of hyper-independence.

Amanda didn't judge me. She didn't tell me I was crazy.

She told me she supported my choice no matter what.

That she didn't want me to throw away a friendship unless I was really ready.

She's always been the voice of reason.

This time was no different.

I decided to write Katherine an email after that.

A final opportunity to say what I needed.

I never heard back from Katherine.

Apparently, we both let go just as easily. Maybe we were supposed to.

I thought Katherine and I would be best friends for the rest of my life.

But it was always supposed to be Amanda.

She always showed up for me. Even when I couldn't show up for her.

When she got pregnant again, this time with a daughter, I didn't react well. I had just lost Katherine as a friend and felt like I was losing Amanda, too.

Instead of being excited for her, I made her pregnancy about me. About how I would miss my drinking partner. My adventure buddy.

We didn't talk for several months after that. Amanda was hurt. Understandably. And I was too selfish to notice.

But unlike Katherine, Amanda's absence felt like a deep void. Like losing a sibling.

I've had a lot of people come in and out of my life. Walked away from dozens of people. Family members, friends, partners. I always knew I would be fine on my own.

But not with her.

I couldn't walk away from Amanda. She's the only person I've ever asked to be back in my life after they've left.

Amanda had every reason to stay mad at me. I showed her a selfish side of me. Thoughtless. Not good.

But she knew it wasn't the real me.

She knew I had reacted from a wounded place. She didn't know how wounded, but she knew enough to see past it.

She forgave me like it was nothing. And we picked up right where we left off.

Amanda's presence in my life feels a lot like Jason's. Like solid ground.

The stability needed to stand.

She balances me.

She doesn't let me wallow in self-pity, but she reminds me it's okay to be upset. It's okay to feel sad about what I've experienced.

But it's not okay to let it drive my life.

Amanda is one of the people who made getting help easier. She never judged me or saw me as weak. The opposite, actually. She saw me as strong.

She helped me reframe asking for help as strength. She helped me orient my thinking toward empowerment.

I've had the honor and privilege of watching her embody it. To sit in her power even when it's hard. To choose growth even when it's hard. She became my model of healing. She became my model of strength.

I've watched Amanda wrestle with her insecurities. After her divorce. After failed relationships.

I sat with her while her heart broke, and I watched her put it back together again. Knowing her value. Never compromising her beliefs to feel loved. Never shrinking to feel loved.

She knew what it took me a long time to learn: If you have to shrink to be loved, then that's not love. It's control.

I've watched Amanda pick herself up over and over again. Always moving forward. Always making herself stronger.

She doesn't want to be stronger. I understand that.

But she alchemizes her pain. Turns it into fuel. Uses it to love herself more.

I didn't have any examples of what profound, deep self-love looked like growing up. I didn't have an example until I met her. And it's one of the most beautiful things I've ever seen.

She's been one of my greatest teachers. She doesn't even know. Probably wouldn't believe it if I told her.

But she makes me better. Every day.

Amanda is my greatest mirror—reflecting back not just the truth of who I am, but the possibility of who I could be.

She isn't just a source of stability.

Amanda is a lighthouse.

She's proof that healing isn't just possible—it's inevitable when you choose yourself.

She's proof that self-love isn't just a choice—it's a birthright.

She's proof that standing tall in your worth isn't just within reach.

It's the only way forward.

Brandi

Brandi knew we would be friends the first time she met me.

I interviewed for a job, and she sat on the panel. I finished answering questions and left.

"Whether we hire her or not," she told the people in the room, "I want to be her friend." That was her feedback on my interview.

I found that out much later. But she always knew. I got the job. My classroom was across the hall from hers. We talked every day, multiple times a day. There was a shorthand between us. An unspoken understanding.

The trauma in her could see the trauma in me, and vice versa.

We never talked about it explicitly, but we understood one another on a different level. Like fluency in a silent language we learned by going through the fires of hell.

I never had to explain myself to her. She just got me.

She loved me from the beginning.

And to be loved by Brandi was special.

She had the kind of spirit that was a magnet for everyone, but especially the wounded. Whether it was adults like me or kids in the building, she became everything to everyone. And she never minded.

She loved people wholly, fully, without question. It was her superpower.

Brandi and I went on trips together. Registered for conferences for professional development. Sometimes we actually went. Other times, we didn't.

We'd play in a new city, making memories together instead.

Brandi always talked about her daughters, the center of her world. Everything she did was for them.

Her face lit up when she talked about them.

Their milestones became moments in my life.

When Sarah got into architecture school. When Mimi graduated high school.

Brandi couldn't wait to tell everyone. The love radiating out of her felt like magic—like basking in the warmth of the sun without worrying about a sunburn.

She understood me without me ever having to say a word.

She always knew when something was off, when I had retreated deep within myself. And she would use humor to bring me back.

We both had the humor of middle school boys. Giggling at double entendres. Finding the dark humor when things were hard.

She was a fierce feminist. In part because she wanted a better world for her girls. In part because she knew the weight of a world that devalues women.

She loved *Harry Potter*. Read every book. Watched the movies on repeat.

Brandi was a force. A light. A rare kind of magic.

Brandi's classroom was *Harry Potter*-themed—every detail meticulously prepared. She ensured its accuracy, down to the smallest touches.

She created hidey-holes for overstimulated students, spaces where they could take a break when the world felt too loud. She understood the power of solitude and built her classroom to accommodate it.

Brandi had one of the most infectious laughs.

One time, we were at Starbucks in the airport, getting coffee. She didn't always have the best awareness of her body in space, which meant she bumped into things a lot.

On this particular day, she knocked over an entire tray of gift cards.

Dozens of them.

Scattered everywhere.

She instantly started laughing, and I did, too.

She dropped to her knees, scrambling to pick up the cards, snorting from laughter, worried she might pee her pants.

The Starbucks barista came around the counter to help, but like me, he wasn't much use. We couldn't stop laughing at Brandi—not in a cruel way, but in that endearing kind of way, when life feels wholesome and light.

Brandi had a way with people.

She could disarm anyone.

She disarmed me.

I've never understood how she did it—how she got past an armor almost no one else could.

And she made it look easy.

Brandi created herself a door and walked right through it.

No one else had ever done that before.

Even with Jason, it took a minute.

But not with her.

I would have to hold her hand on the plane. She hated to fly. She would take anxiety medicine, sometimes vodka—anything to keep herself calm. But mostly, she would just hold my hand.

Anytime the plane shook, she would grab on, and I would squeeze tighter, letting her know she was safe. That I had her.

One time, we were supposed to go to a conference in Boston, but we skipped it. Instead, we went to Salem. Spent the day doing witchy things—walking through cemeteries, exploring spell shops, talking about the historic oppression of women.

She listened to Eminem when she needed to calm herself down. Knew every word of his old stuff. It was her hype music, her tool for feeling brave.

She was my hype person.

Whatever big dream I had, she championed it.

No judgment. No doubt. Just belief.

Every single time.

I have a voicemail on my phone.

It wasn't anything special. Just something about school. But she ended it the way we always ended our calls.

"Love you."

I had no idea how important that voicemail would become.

Two days later, Brandi had a stroke.

She was way too young.

They got her to the hospital, ran tests, and found out she had a brain condition she likely didn't even know about.

Moyamoya.

She was in the ICU for two weeks. Her daughters stayed by her side every minute of visiting hours, giving me updates, letting me know how she was doing, what the doctors were saying.

I begged the universe for a miracle. *Just let her be okay.*

Her blood pressure was high. The doctors worried about more strokes.

She needed surgery, but she wasn't stable enough yet.

She never would be.

Instead, she continued to deteriorate, suffering a series of strokes at night that left her brain-dead.

Her daughters—both college students—were now tasked with making an impossible decision.

They had to let their mom go.

She was still on life support. They were going to donate her organs.

Brandi's final gift.

I was at her school when I found out, training her long-term sub on how to take care of Brandi's kids the way Brandi would.

My stomach was uneasy.

My body was already preparing for a truth my mind would struggle to accept.

Tamara, her best friend, called.

The decision had been made. The transplant team would assemble.

Brandi was going to die that day.

November 8, 2021.

I became hysterical, shaking, crying.

Staff at Brandi's school called my husband. He picked me up at the school. The principal and another teacher guided me out the side door, so the kids wouldn't see me fall apart.

As soon as I saw Jason get out of the car, I ran to him, collapsed into his arms, and started wailing.

The kind of wailing I had heard in the ER all those years ago.

Brandi's daughters told me I could come to the hospital, sit with them, say goodbye.

So we went.

Sat there in a stunned state.

The world didn't make sense anymore.

Like it had been tipped on its axis.

Occasionally, we broke the tension by telling stories about Brandi— her humor, her love.

Other times, we just sat and cried.

After Brandi's parents said their goodbyes, it was my turn.

I went into her room. Jason went with me.

I sat in the chair beside her bed.

She was hooked up to tubes, but she looked like she was sleeping.

She looked at peace.

I held her hand, told her over and over how much I loved her.

How grateful I was for her friendship.

How grateful I was to love her.

I squeezed her hand tightly. Just like on the plane.

I wanted her to know she was okay.

She was held.

She was safe.

When it was time to leave, I kissed her forehead, thanked her for being my friend.

For choosing me.

Eventually, I knew I had to go.

To walk out of her hospital room. To never see her again.

The weight of the moment pressed against my chest.

Every step toward the door felt heavier.

I turned, looked back, and blew her a kiss.

A few hours later, attendants wheeled her to the operating room to retrieve her organs.

Doctors and nurses lined the hall to honor her gift.

A sendoff fit for a heroine.

For Brandi.

I felt it immediately—the void in my heart where she was supposed to be.

Nothing made sense.

How could she be gone?

How could I lose one of the only people I've ever let see me?

After the funeral, I felt numb.

Stunned the world still could exist without her.

Stunned *I* still could.

I didn't know how to process her death.

I had never lost a friend before.

Let alone one who made me feel safe.

I shut down.

Hid within myself.

Uncertain how to navigate this grief.

The very person I would ask, the one who would have the answers, was the one I was grieving.

I would stare off into space.

Not thinking about anything.

Not present.

Empty.

A Brandi-sized hole in my heart that could never be filled.

The memories of her were both beautiful and painful.

And within weeks of going back to work, people stopped talking about her.

Stopped asking me about her.

The world moved on so easily.

Just kept going.

But I was stuck.

A few weeks after Brandi's death was her birthday.

I was angry that day.

She was supposed to be alive to celebrate her birthday.

I was supposed to celebrate her.

But I didn't feel much like celebrating.

How could someone so good and so wonderful be taken so early?

How could the world not even understand what it had lost?

Part of me wanted to shake people and scream at them—

Don't you understand how unfair this is? Doesn't it make you angry?

But I never did.

I just kept putting one foot in front of the other.

Kept moving forward.

Kept breathing.

In February 2022, four months after her death, I sat in a meditation class.

The teacher shared a quote from Buddhist monk Thich Nhat Hanh.

"Many people are alive, but don't touch the miracle of being alive."

The words hit me like an exhale I didn't know I was holding.

I sat there, heart pounding, hands gripping my knees. Letting the words settle.

I said them out loud to myself.

"Many people are alive, but don't touch the miracle of being alive."

My stomach dropped. My breath caught.

I knew it was a message from Brandi.

A reminder to keep living.

To love life the way she did.

To love others the way she did.

The quote made me remember a conversation I had with her a few months before she died.

She had asked about my therapist.

She could see the changes in me from the work I was doing.

She said I seemed lighter.

Like the world didn't feel so heavy anymore.

She was right.

She asked me for my therapist's name.

Said if I trusted them, that was enough for her.

She was ready to face her shit and let it go.

She was ready to live life more fully.

More healed.

I gave her Brittni's number.

She told me she would call.

She never got the chance.

After the meditation class ended, I sat there, talking to Brandi.

I made a promise to her.

I promised to do what she didn't get to—heal.

I promised to live fully.

To love loudly.

To take her with me everywhere I went.

I've never met anyone like her.

I'm fairly confident I never will again.

There was only one Brandi.

And like the characters of *Harry Potter*, she was pure magic.

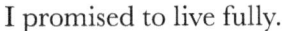

I wipe the tears from my eyes. "She was incredible, 30s Me. All three of these women are."

"Yeah. I'm pretty fucking lucky to know them."

"You know what's amazing?"

"What's that?"

"They were your teachers. But you were also theirs."

I watch 30s Me process what I said. Her head tilts slightly. She starts blinking quickly. I can tell she's trying the idea on for size, seeing how it fits her.

"Maybe."

I knew she'd resist. I still struggle to believe it sometimes.

"You know what I think is amazing?"

"What?"

"Each of them gave me something different. Brittni taught me how to heal. Amanda showed me how to stand tall in my worth. And Brandi—"

30s Me swallows hard.

"Brandi taught me how to live."

I smile. "Three wise women."

"The wisest."

We sit in comfortable silence, the weight of their lessons settling around us like a well-worn quilt.

They are woven into me now.

Brittni's patience. Amanda's steadiness. Brandi's light.

They don't just hold me up—they carry me forward.

30s Me exhales, glancing over at me. *"So. What now?"*

I smile, soft but certain. "Now, I keep going. Taking their lessons with me. Taking them with me."

30s Me smiles, nods, and closes her eyes.

"Make them proud."

She doesn't even open her eyes when she says it.

She already knows I will.

11.

The Reckoning

I sit on my meditation cushion and close my eyes.

I take a few cleansing breaths.

Inhale. Exhale.

Inhale. Exhale.

My stomach twists. My hands twitch in my lap.

I know I need to do this, but the weight of it presses against my chest.

I wait until I feel steady enough.

Then, I call for them.

"Little Me? Teen Me? 20s Me? 30s Me? Can we talk?"

"All of us?" Teen Me sounds skeptical.

"Yes, all of you. I thought we could sit around the table and talk."

My stomach swirls. I have to keep going.

I imagine us all at the table—all except 20s Me. I know she won't come out of the shadows. But I know she's here.

Teen Me leans back in her chair, arms crossed. She glances around at the others before fixing her gaze on me. There's tension in her jaw, like she's holding back. Finally, she exhales sharply.

"What do you even want from us? You dragged us all here. What do you need?"

Of course she's the one to go first.

"A fair question. To be honest, I don't fully know."

I scan their faces, then look back at Teen Me.

"I just know I can't feel whole without you. All of you."

I take a breath.

"You are the keepers of my stories. Sure, I can play
the memories in my mind.
I can even feel them in my body sometimes.
But each of you lived them.
You know them in ways I never fully can.

"Without you, the stories begin to fade.
And if the stories fade…
Parts of me do too.

"I don't want that."

Teen Me narrows her eyes, studying me.

She uncrosses her arms but keeps her hands balled into fists against her legs. She wants to challenge me—she always does—but my answer makes her hesitate.

She tilts her head, considering.

"So you don't want us to disappear. Fine. But where the fuck were you when we needed you?"

I look down immediately. Ashamed.

I want to tell her I never left. That I was always here. But that's simply not true.

"I wish I had a better answer, but the truth is...
I couldn't look at myself.
For so long, I couldn't turn the lens of my awareness
inward.
I was afraid of what I'd find.
Of what I'd have to relive.

"So instead of holding you
the way you deserved—
Instead of thanking you for surviving—
I hid.

"I was a coward.

"But I'm here now.

"I've finally stopped hiding."

Teen Me lets out a sharp breath through her nose. She looks away, biting the inside of her cheek. Scratching at her thumbnails.

"Yeah. You stopped hiding. Now that it's safe. Now that it's easy.

"But where the fuck were you when it wasn't?"

She looks back at me, and this time, her voice shakes—not with fear, but with fury.

"You left me to carry it all.

"The shame. The pain. The anger.

"Do you have any idea how fucking heavy it was?"

I immediately look down again. I take a breath, then force myself to look back up. My eyes meet hers.

"I have a pretty good sense of the weight of it.
I also know it hurt you to feel that, yet again, no one
was fighting for you.
I don't expect you to forgive me, Teen Me. But I am hoping
you'll let me explain why I couldn't hold you.
Why I couldn't hold the weight."

Teen Me crosses her arms tightly, jaw clenched. She's still scanning me, like she's waiting for a lie. Like she's daring me to make an excuse.

"Fine." Her voice is clipped, like she doesn't trust herself to say more without it cracking. *"Explain."*

I glance around the table, making sure each version is listening. I need them all to hear what I'm about to say.

"I hated myself. I sometimes still do.
I didn't think I was worthy of anything.
Of love. Of goodness. Of any of you.

"I thought I failed you.

"I couldn't move on. I couldn't move
forward.
The pain of what you carried was so heavy
and so terrifying, I didn't want to feel it.
I didn't want to hurt.

"I thought if I just kept going, just
kept moving forward, kept achieving—
the pain would lessen. That I would feel
like enough.

"But I never did.

"Every degree. Every certification. Every new job.
I kept hoping they would fill the void in me.
The part of me that was calling out
for something. The part I couldn't satisfy.

"What I didn't understand then is that *you* were that part.

"I was trying to fill a void that could only be filled when I stopped
looking outside of myself.

"The emptiness I felt was because I was so disconnected
from you.

"From me."

Tears blur my vision. One slips down my cheek.

Teen Me doesn't respond right away. She's still staring, her eyes
searching mine for something—truth, maybe.

A part of her wants to stay angry. A part of her wants to tell me it's
too late.

But something stops her.

She shifts in her chair, crossing her arms tighter around herself.

*"So now you think you can just come back? After all this time? After leaving me
to carry everything alone?"*

Her voice wavers, just barely. She shakes her head, her grip on her arms like a vice. *"I needed you. And you were gone."*

I nod.

"You're right. I was. I abandoned you
because I thought you would mess up my life.
That the weight you carry would pull me down.
Make it hard to live my life.
But I was wrong.

"By facing you, by helping to carry the weight, by seeing
you through a lens of love—that's how
I can continue to heal."

Teen Me laughs.

"A lens of love?! Are you fucking kidding me?" She rolls her eyes.

"Yeah. For me to stop hating myself,
I have to stop
blaming you."

My muscles tighten. Already bracing for her rage.

Teen Me flinches. Her jaw clenches.

She obviously wants to argue. She wants to snap back.

But she doesn't.

Instead, she looks away, staring at some fixed point in the distance.

"Blame me for what?"

Her voice is quieter now, but there's something sharp underneath it.

She swallows hard, and when she turns back, her expression is unreadable.

"What exactly do you think I did to deserve that?"

I swallow. My throat feels dry.

"I blamed you for not fighting back harder.
For not telling other people.
For not being believed.

"I didn't think you deserved what happened to you,
but I did think you could have done more.

"I was wrong.

"Blaming you was easier than accepting the truth."

Teen Me lets out a sharp, bitter laugh.

She shakes her head, eyes flashing with something between fury and heartbreak.

"You thought I could have done more?"

Her voice rises. She leans forward, elbows on the table, staring me down.

"You think I didn't want to? You think I didn't fucking try?"

She exhales hard through her nose, shaking her head again.

"You have no idea what it was like to live inside my body, do you? You have no idea how hard I tried to keep us safe."

Her grip tightens on the edge of the table, knuckles turning white.

"And you—" She swallows hard, her voice breaking. *"You were supposed to be the one who finally saw me. And you—"*

She chokes on the words.

"You didn't."

I nod again.

"You're right. I didn't. I didn't want to.

Seeing you meant I would not only have to sit with what happened
to you—
I would also have to tell you what I know now.

"That none of what happened to you was about you.

"It happened to you.
But it wasn't about you.
And it wasn't because of you."

I brace myself again.

Teen Me flinches, like the words hit her physically. Her hands curl
into fists on the table. She looks away, her jaw tight, breath quickening.

"Don't."

Her voice is low. A warning.

"Don't try to make this make sense.
Don't try to wrap it up in something neat.
It's not neat."

She shakes her head, blinking hard.

"You don't get to tell me it wasn't about me.

"Because it felt like it was about me.
Every fucking second of it.

"It felt like it was my fault.
Like I asked for it.
Like I was disposable."

She swallows, her throat bobbing.

"And when I needed someone to tell me it wasn't?

"No one did."

Her eyes flick back to me. Sharp. Accusing.

"Not even you."

I take a moment. More tears fall from my eyes. Her words land like daggers.

"I know.
I couldn't be what you needed me to be then.
But I can now.
And I'm not trying to wrap it up into something neat.
What you experienced was so fucking terrible.
You didn't deserve any of it.
You deserved to be believed."

I exhale. The weight of it all pressing into me.

"I wish I could have been better for you.
I wish I didn't disappoint you.
That I was more healed for you.

"I am trying.

"Every single fucking day, I am trying.

"I know I can't go back and undo the hurt I've caused,
but I can promise you this:
I am not going to hurt you again."

Teen Me studies me, eyes scanning my face like she's searching for a lie.

Her arms stay crossed, her posture still stiff, but something in her expression shifts—just a fraction.

She exhales sharply through her nose.

"You're saying that like it's supposed to make a difference."

I don't say anything.

I just let the words sit.

She chews the inside of her cheek, jaw tense.

"Do you even know what it's like to carry this alone?"

She gestures between us, her voice quieter now.

"Do you know what it's like to be trapped in it?
To have no one tell you it's going to be okay?
To have no one tell you you're not a piece of shit
when that's all your mind can tell you?"

Her voice is thick with something she won't name.

She scratches at her thumbnails.

"I needed someone to fucking see me. And no one did."

Her lip quivers. She bites it to stop it.

She blinks fast, looking up. Then back at me.

Her voice drops lower.

"Do you see me now?"

I soften my face. Try to blink back my tears, but they keep falling anyway.

"Yes. I see you now.
You are the fire within me.
The one who keeps me moving forward.

"You're relentless.

"You can sit in your power, and it does not scare you.

"I'm jealous of that."

Teen Me rolls her eyes.

"You use sarcasm as a defense mechanism.
A shield for what's happening under the surface.

"You're scared.

"You have plenty of reasons to be,
but what scares you the most is the anger you feel.

"You have only known to be afraid of anger.
It has always caused you to get hurt.

So, you don't allow yourself to feel the anger.
Not fully.

"But it slips out at times—
in your body language, in your tone of voice—
it's constantly brewing deep within you.

"You want to scream.
You want to break things.

"You want the people who hurt you to feel your pain.
You want retribution.

"And you feel guilty for that.

"Because good people shouldn't wish harm on others.

"So, you don't trust yourself to handle anger.

"Instead of expressing it, you blame yourself
for having angry thoughts.

"You think you're failing.
That you're a bad person.

"And you won't believe anyone who tells you otherwise.

"Including me."

Teen Me goes still. Completely still.

Like a predator who's been spotted.

Like she's deciding whether to attack or retreat.

Her jaw clenches. Her hands fist at her sides.

"Fuck you."

Her voice is quiet, but the rage in it is sharp enough to slice.

I don't flinch. I don't move.

I just nod.

"Yeah."

Her nostrils flare.

She looks away, her breathing uneven.

Her fingers flex—like she wants to throw a punch. Like she wants to destroy something just to see if she still has the power to.

Her voice wobbles, but the anger doesn't leave.

"I don't need you to analyze me."

Her eyes flash when she finally meets my gaze.

"I don't need you to fucking tell me what I feel. I KNOW what I feel."

I nod again.

"I know you do."

She swallows hard.

"Then why say it?"

I exhale, slow and steady.

"Because you deserve to hear the truth about yourself.

"And the truth is, you're not a bad person, Teen Me."

She flinches.

A full-body reaction.

Like the words landed right in the center of her.

Her fists clench again. She shakes her head, but she doesn't speak.

I lean forward, voice gentle but unwavering.

"You're allowed to be angry."

Her throat bobs.

She shakes her head harder, like she's trying to shake the words loose before they stick.

I don't let her escape them.

"You're allowed to be furious.
You're allowed to want justice.
That doesn't make you bad."

Teen Me's voice wavers, just barely.

"But what if I can't control it?"

She doesn't look at me when she says it.

She just stares at her hands.

"What if it eats me alive?"

I exhale, slow and steady.

"It won't."

I let the words settle before I continue.

"Because it hasn't.
You're still here."

Her breathing is ragged now.

Her shoulders shake, just slightly.

Her eyes squeeze shut.

I stay silent.

Let her sit with it.

Let her fight it if she needs to.

Finally, her voice comes out hoarse. Small.

"I don't want to be like them."

I swallow the lump in my throat.

"You're nothing like them."

Her shoulders tremble harder.

I lean in, just slightly.

"You are angry because you were hurt.
But you are not hurting others.

"That's the difference.

"That's the part that matters."

Her breath quivers.

Her fists hesitantly unfurl.

Her shoulders drop.

She doesn't say anything.

But for the first time, she doesn't look like she wants to run.

Teen Me looks at me for a long time.

Too long.

I know that look.

She's testing me.

"So that's it?" she finally says. *"You show up now, and I'm just supposed to believe you? Just supposed to trust that you won't leave me again?"*

She leans back in her chair, arms crossing tighter.

"Because I don't. I don't trust you."

I swallow hard.

"I know."

Her jaw tightens.

"Then why even bother?"

I don't look away.

I hold her gaze.

Hold the weight of her question.

"Because I don't need you to trust me yet," I say.

"I just need you to let me try."

Her eyes flick away, just for a second.

Maybe she's considering it.

Maybe she's not.

I can't tell.

But she doesn't get up.

She doesn't walk away.

Teen Me looks away—

but she doesn't leave.

She stays in her chair.

That's enough for me, for now.

The silence stretches—thick, but not as sharp as before.

Then, suddenly, Little Me's voice breaks it.

"Can it be someone else's turn now?!"

I smile.

"Of course. What's on your mind, Little Me?"

She spins in her chair.

Her pink dress has splashes of mud on it.

I giggle under my breath.

She always made messes.

Some things never change.

Her eyes flit up to mine, then back to her feet.

I wonder if she heard my laugh.

Her fingers twist at the hem of her shirt, tugging, picking—nervous energy looking for an escape.

"I don't get it."

Her voice is small, but there's an edge of frustration underneath.

She lifts her head, her eyes searching mine, like she's desperate for an answer that will make it all make sense.

"You're saying you're here to be with us.
That you're sorry you weren't before.

"But why should we forgive you?"

Her breath quickens, like she's realizing just how much she has to say.

"You knew I was scared.
You knew I was hurting.
But you left me there too.

"You left me in the dark with the weight of her."

Her voice catches, but she swallows it down.

"I was just a kid.
And you abandoned me.

You made me think you didn't believe me.
That I wasn't good enough for you."

She spins slightly in the chair.

Her fingernails dig into her palms now, pressing crescents into her skin.

There are tears in her eyes.

"How am I supposed to believe you're here now? That you'll actually stay?"

Her voice shakes, but she doesn't seem to care.

She stares at me, waiting.

Waiting for proof.

Waiting for me to give her something real.

I steady myself.

Choose my words carefully.

"I can't answer that for you, Little Me.
I can't make you believe me.
All I can do is be here now.
And keep being here.
The believing part is up to you.
Whenever you are ready to believe me—
I will still be here."

Little Me's bottom lip quivers.

She looks down again, her small hands still clenched into fists, her shoulders drawn up like she's trying to make herself smaller—like she's trying to disappear.

"That's what grown-ups always say," she mumbles, barely above a whisper. *"That they'll be there. That they won't leave."*

She lifts her gaze.

And there's something in her expression—

like she's torn between wanting to trust me and knowing better.

"But they always do."

Her voice breaks on the last word.

She sucks in a sharp breath, pressing her lips together like she's trying to swallow her own feelings before they spill out.

Tears fall down her face.

"Even you."

She shakes her head, taking a small step back.

"I don't want to need you.
Because what if I do?

"What if I start believing you—
and you change your mind?

"What if one day you decide I'm too much?"

Her arms wrap tightly around herself.

"Or not enough?

"I don't think I can survive that again."

She stares at me, waiting. Her brown eyes pleading.

Needing me to be different.

Needing me to mean it this time.

I inhale deeply.

"Little Me. I know you're scared.
I know you don't want to get hurt again.
You've been hurt a lot already.
Had to grow up before you should have.
I understand why you're afraid to let anyone in."

I let my words sit with her for a moment.

Her eyes never break my gaze.

"But here's the thing—
I am working on getting better.
When I hurt you before,
I was hurting too.
I still am.
But I am starting to see the lies others told us about our worth.
The ways our trauma has lied to us.
I left you before because I didn't have the space to hold you.
But now I do.

"That doesn't mean I will get it right 100% of the time,
But it does mean I want to try."

Teen Me looks up. Watching. Listening.

Little Me sways in her seat slightly. Like she's letting my words settle in.

Her fingers still fidget at the hem of her shirt.

Her brows knit together.

She exhales, slow and shaky.

"I want to believe you," she admits, her voice barely above a whisper.

"But...I don't know how."

Her eyes flick down again.

And when she speaks next, it's like she's confessing something she hasn't even admitted, even to herself.

"I don't know what it feels like to be safe."

She blinks fast. More tears filling her eyes.

"I've never felt it. Not really. Not in a way that lasted."

Her arms tighten around herself.

A shield.

A barrier.

A last line of defense.

*"And if I don't know what it feels like…
How will I ever know if you're really giving it to me?"*

She looks up, something desperate in her expression now.

Not anger.

Not even doubt.

Just…longing.

"How will I know I'm safe?"

I feel the weight of her question.

Deep within me.

Like it's written on my bones.

I give her a knowing smile.

"You won't always know it. But you'll feel it.
The moments when it's okay to put the armor down.
To not be so guarded.

"You might not notice them right away.
And when you do notice them,
you won't trust them.

But the more you feel it, the more you'll ease into it.

"I still struggle to feel safe.
I still struggle to trust the feeling.

"But I've felt it enough to know—
I want more of it.
And less of how I feel without it."

Little Me shifts her weight in her chair.

Her small fingers still clenched around the fabric of her dress.

She looks down, biting her lip. Considering my words.

Finally, she mumbles,

"I don't know if I can do that."

She sniffles, rubbing at her nose with the back of her hand.

"I don't know how to put the armor down.
It's part of me now.
If I let go of it…
What's left?"

She looks up at me, eyes wide.

Full of something fragile but brave.

"If I stop being strong…then who am I?"

I smile and reach for her.

"Oh, Little Me.
You are so much more.
You became strong out of necessity.
Out of survival.

"But that is not all you are.

"You are my foundation.
The spark of joy and love inside me—
The part of me that has kept going when things were hard.

"You are a light in my darkness.

"You're my *why*.

"I want to give you the life you deserved—
but didn't get to experience.
I want to make you proud. All of you."

I gesture around the table.

Little Me just stares at me.

Her small hands clenched. Her lips pressed into a thin line—

like she's trying to keep herself from believing.

From hoping.

From letting this in.

Then, finally, she whispers,

"But I don't even know how to be proud."

She swallows hard.

Her little shoulders rise and fall with a shaky breath.

"No one ever showed me how."

Her eyes search mine.

Full of something unspoken.

A need she doesn't know how to name.

"Will you teach me?"

I smile broadly.

Let out a deep exhale.

"It would be my honor, Little Me."

I keep my eyes locked on hers until she looks away.

She goes back to spinning in the chair.

I glance around the table.

Teen Me is still lost in thought.

30s Me leans back in her chair, rubbing her temples.

She exhales through her nose, slow and measured—like she's trying to hold herself together.

Not out of fear.

Not out of avoidance.

Just…exhaustion.

She finally lifts her head, eyes landing on me—not with resistance, not with anger, but with something else.

Something heavier.

"I'm so fucking tired."

Her voice isn't sharp.

It isn't accusing.

It's just…weary.

She tilts her head slightly, studying me.

Not unkind, just skeptical.

"I've been doing the work.
I showed up when no one else did.
I started digging through the wreckage, trying
to make sense of it all.
And I kept thinking—

"If I just work hard enough, if I just keep going,
one day it won't be so hard."

She sighs, shifting in her seat.

"But it's still hard."

She shakes her head, running a hand through her short hair.

"I just want to know…does it ever get easier?"

I give her a knowing nod.

"It does. Just not like you think."

I wait for her eyes to stay with mine before continuing.

"It's not that it gets easier.
It's that you learn to hold it differently.
All the awfulness becomes something that happened to you—
but not something that feels like it's still happening to you.

"You don't feel it in your body the same way.
You won't tense up as much.
You won't jump at loud noises as often.
You learn to live with the pain,
but not let it consume you."

30s Me exhales, slow and deep—like she's letting my words move through her.

Making sure they are the truth.

She nods, just barely.

Like she wants to believe me—but there's still something unsettled behind her eyes.

"I've heard that before," she says, her voice quiet, contemplative.

"That healing isn't about erasing the pain—
It's about carrying it differently."

She leans forward slightly, resting her elbows on the table.

Rubbing her hands together absently.

"But what if I don't want to carry it at all?"

She tilts her head, searching my face.

Not accusing.

Just…asking.

"I didn't break me. Other people did.
But I have to clean up their mess.

"It's just not fair."

30s Me starts to pick at her thumbnails.

She looks down at her feet.

"I know you're saying it won't feel as sharp.
That it won't feel like it's still happening.

"But does it ever leave?"

She swallows hard, her voice dropping lower.

"Or am I always going to feel it, just in different ways?"

I hear the quiet desperation in her voice.

Begging me to give her hope.

Unsure what to do with it if I did.

I reach for her hand.

Squeeze it gently.

"It's always going to be there.
It's a part of you. Of us. Of our story.
We can't change that. Even if we want to.
But we decide how much power we give it.
How much we let it take from us."

30s Me tightens her fingers around mine, just for a second.

Not in resistance—

more like she's needing something solid to hold onto.

She nods slowly, lips pressing together.

She's listening.

She's absorbing.

Finally, she lets out a breath that sounds like she's been holding it for years.

"I think that's the part I'm the most afraid of," she admits.

"That I don't know how to let it take up less space.
That if I stop letting it define me...
I won't know who I am without it."

Her voice shakes, just barely.

"I built my whole identity around surviving.
Around holding it all together.

Around pushing through.
If I stop…
If I really start letting it go…
Then who the fuck am I?"

Her fingers flex around mine again, and when she meets my eyes—

she's not challenging me.

She's pleading with me.

I smile, gently.

I can tell she's scared.

I want to reassure her.

I take a breath, exhaling out of my mouth.

"That's the magic of healing.
Instead of letting our trauma decide for us,
we get to uncover it—one piece at a time.
I've learned some pieces are harder to love than others,
but I can understand them more.
I know why they're there.

"Healing is an ongoing process.
It's not clean.
And it's certainly not easy.
But it's the only way forward."

I look at her.

Slumped in the chair.

She stares down at her hands.

Her eyes, heavy and worn out.

"You know what else I know?"

She looks up at me.

Waits for me to answer.

"It's working."

30s Me stills.

She blinks, once—

like she's not sure she heard me right.

Like she doesn't know whether to believe it.

Then she lets out a shaky breath, her shoulders dropping just slightly.

"It is?"

Her voice is quiet.

Like she's afraid to let herself hope.

Like she doesn't trust the thought yet.

But there's something else in her face now—

a flicker of something lighter.

Something softer.

She presses her lips together.

Looks away for a second.

Then meets my eyes again.

"I don't always feel it," she admits.

*"Most days, it still feels like I'm wading through the same shit.
Like I'm stuck."*

She exhales.

Shakes her head.

*"But you're saying…I'm actually moving forward?
That it's doing something?"*

There's no sarcasm in her tone.

No disbelief.

Just raw, cautious curiosity.

Like she wants so badly to believe me.

"Yes, it's doing something.
When you made the choice to go to therapy,
you made the choice for every future
version of you to live differently.
To carry the weight of our trauma differently.
Because of you, the work is working.
Because of you, *we are healing.*"

30s Me sits back in her chair.

Closes her eyes.

Takes a deep breath.

A rare look of satisfaction settles on her face.

I recognize it immediately.

I gesture to Little Me.

She stops spinning in the chair.

I silently mouth the words, "That's pride."

Her face lights up.

She covers her mouth.

Holding in her excitement.

We let 30s Me enjoy this moment.

She's earned it.

I turn my attention to 20s Me.

She stays in the shadows.

She isn't like the others.

She doesn't push back like Teen Me.

She doesn't plead like Little Me.

She doesn't search for proof like 30s Me.

She hides.

But I can feel her there.

And I know exactly why she's in the shadows.

She isn't waiting for reassurance.

She isn't waiting to be told she did the best she could.

She's waiting for the blow.

The one that says it's her fault.

Because that's what she's used to.

She believes she deserves it.

Finally, after a long stretch of silence, she speaks.

Her voice is flat.

Not emotionless.

But hollow.

She learned to keep herself small enough to go unnoticed.

"I already know what you think of me. You don't have to say it out loud."

There is a deep unease to her.

I feel it in my heart.

"I was the one who made all the wrong choices.
I was the one who should have known better.
And I didn't."

She exhales.

It sounds sharp.

Bitter.

"So, what is there to say?"

She finally steps into the light of my awareness.

But not all the way.

Just enough for me to barely see her.

She sits on the edge of my visibility, slumped over.

Her head hanging.

She looks like a sad puppy in a cartoon.

She's thin.

Anxiety has stolen her appetite for years.

Her face is flat.

Empty.

There's no anger.

No fight.

No hope for redemption.

Just acceptance.

She has already condemned herself.

And she's convinced I have, too.

"Just say it.
Say I ruined us.
I destroyed our life.
Say it, because at least then I'll know
I was right."

My eyes immediately fill with tears.

"You're right.
I blame you.
I do.
I wish I didn't, but I do."

20s Me doesn't flinch.

She nods.

Once.

She expected that answer.

She's been expecting it for years.

She exhales through her nose, slow and measured.

Her fingers grip the fabric of her black, Queen T-shirt.

"I know."

Her voice doesn't waver.

There's no protest.

No argument.

Just quiet acceptance.

"I blame me, too."

She lets out a hollow laugh, shaking her head.

"It's funny, isn't it?
How I thought I was making the best choices I could?
How I thought I was doing what I had to do?
And now, here we are."

Her voice is tired.

Not in the way 30s Me was—this is different.

This is the exhaustion of someone who has already lost.

Of someone who already feels broken.

She finally lifts her head fully.

Meets my gaze for the first time.

"So, what do you want from me?"

Her eyes search mine.

But she already knows the answer.

"An apology?"

She lets out another empty laugh.

But there's no amusement behind it.

"Fine.
I'm sorry.
I'm sorry I fucked everything up.
I'm sorry I ruined our life.
I'm sorry I was weak."

Her voice cracks on the last word.

But she swallows it down.

She sits there.

Arms crossing tightly over her chest.

Her entire body braced.

Locked in place.

Ready to survive whatever comes next.

"There. Now what?"

I look at her for a few breaths.

The silence is uncomfortable for both of us.

My face feels warm.

Tears stream down my face.

I take a few breaths to settle myself.

She's watching me.

She can tell I'm struggling.

"Just say it. Say what you need to say."

I look down.

Wipe my eyes with my sleeve.

"I blame you because it's easier than the truth.
I don't want to accept that at any point, I
could have done things differently.
I could have made a different choice.
One that would have made life easier
for my son.
But I didn't.
You may have made the choice to let him go over there
50 percent of the time—
But I am the one who kept letting him go."

20s Me stills.

Her breathing halts.

Just for a second.

The weight of my words landed exactly where they were meant to.

She blinks once.

Then again.

Her lips part—like she might say something.

But she doesn't.

Because what is there to say?

She looks away, her jaw tightening, her fingers curling against her arms—nails digging into her skin.

When she speaks, her voice is barely audible.

"So, it wasn't just me."

She lets out a shaky breath, her shoulders trembling slightly.

"You made the same choice I did."

She shakes her head, eyes flickering with something deep and gut-wrenching.

She's bracing herself.

"I thought it was just me, but you're saying you failed him, too?"

She's expecting me to take it back.

To say she misunderstood me.

I don't say a word.

We sit in silence.

I can tell she's trying to make sense of it all.

"You did it, too, but you still hate me for it."

Her voice cracks, but she doesn't try to cover it.

She looks at me again.

Her eyes red-rimmed.

Tired.

"So, how do you live with that?"

Her voice is quiet.

"Because I don't know how."

I take a moment.

My hands shake.

My breath becomes shallow.

I try to settle myself.

"I don't hate you, 20s Me.

I blame you for the choice you made,
because I am not ready to face
my ongoing culpability.

"Don't you get it?

I didn't make the same choice as you, 20s Me—
I made worse ones.
I had more information than you did,
more resources than you,
more stability,
more fight—
and I *still* didn't do anything."

20s Me stares at me.

Her breath hitches.

And for the first time—

she looks unsteady.

She leans back.

Regains her balance.

Takes a deep breath and looks at me.

Really looks at me.

And then—

she shakes her head.

"No."

Her voice is barely there.

"Don't do that."

She grips her body tighter.

"Don't sit there and tell me
you were worse than me.
That you had more and still—"

She swallows, hard.

"I know what you're doing.
You think if you take all the blame,
it makes it easier for me.
That if you carry the weight of it,
I don't have to."

Her breath is shaky.

And when she finally speaks again, her voice is raw, stripped bare of any emotion.

"But I already carry it.
I already feel it.
Every. Fucking. Day."

She presses the heel of her palm into her eyes.

Her breath is uneven.

"And you—you're telling me you do, too?"

Her hands drop to the sides of her body.

Like she doesn't know what to do with them.

Like she's realizing something she never let herself believe before.

She lets out a breath—

one that sounds just like mine.

Her voice is small.

"Then we've both been carrying it alone."

She swallows.

Blinking up at me.

Her breath stutters.

Like she doesn't know if she's allowed to say it.

Like she's afraid to believe it.

And then—

barely above a whisper—

"And maybe...we don't have to anymore."

12.

Arrows

The others left me with my own thoughts after they stepped out of my awareness.

I used to run from moments like this—when I wasn't trying to be more or do more.

It always made me uncomfortable because that's when the monster in my mind came calling.

Telling me all the ways I failed. All the ways I am a burden. All the ways I am not a good person.

I hated it.

I used to feed the monster, helpless to stop it. But now I see it for what it really is.

A couple of years ago, I sat in a meditation class, a five-day silent retreat, done entirely online. Only the teacher was allowed to speak.

She gave two lessons each day—Dharma talks. Ancient wisdom meant to help ease our suffering. The talks were short. Quick little nuggets for reflection.

One day, the teacher shared the parable of the two arrows from the Buddha, and it changed everything for me.

The Buddha once said that every person has two arrows.

The first arrow is the pain itself—the wound that comes from loss, betrayal, failure, or rejection. This arrow is universal. No one escapes it.

The second arrow?

That one, we fire ourselves.

It's the stories we attach to the pain of the first arrow—the self-blame, the shame, the relentless questioning of, *What if I had done something different?*

The second arrow is overthinking, self-doubt, the belief that because something bad happened, we must have deserved it.

The Buddha said the first arrow is inevitable.

The second arrow is optional.

I think about this parable every single day.

I wish I could say I've learned how to stop firing the second arrow altogether.

I still pick it up. I still shoot it.

Some days, I don't even realize I'm doing it until I'm already bleeding.

I've also learned something else.

I can put the arrow down.

And when I pick it up again—because I will—I can put it down again.

Over and over and over.

Next to yoga, this parable has been my saving grace.

When I feel anxious or when I'm cruel to myself, I ask, *Is this a second arrow?*

Most of the time, the answer is yes.

So I put it down. I shift my thinking.

It's not always easy. And it doesn't mean I won't pick up the second arrow five minutes later. But I stop myself long enough to put it down.

And I will put it down over and over and over again.

By identifying my second arrows, I am learning to ease my own suffering.

Distrust

Distrust is the second arrow that never misses.

I don't trust Jason's unconditional love—*love should have a cost.*

I don't trust my friends to hold my story—*they'll drop it, eventually.*

I don't trust myself to choose right—*what if I ruin everything?*

Distrust is a wall. A weight. A waiting game.

It feels like immediate resistance. Like there's something left unsaid.

Like an invisible wall around me. A wall I have in place all the time but only notice when I'm skeptical—of someone. Of myself.

When I'm expecting it all to fall apart. When I'm making plans for how it will.

I feel it in my gut. An unease, like something's not right. I become hyper-aware. Noticing every subtle shift in body language. Every change in tone. Every thought in my mind. A code I must break to find the truth.

When I struggle to trust myself, my body freezes. I don't know what to do next, so I just hold still—waiting for the answer to come.

Distrust feels normal.

It's a script within me, running exactly as programmed.

When I try to challenge it, it only gets louder.

Jason offers me love without conditions—love I didn't have to earn—but I still look for the catch. And when nothing comes, when there's no price to be paid, I can't wrap my head around it. It doesn't make sense. I don't trust it. I try to reject it.

The magic of Jason is that he knows this. He trusts that I won't stay in that fearful place for too long. He trusts my ability to accept something even when I don't understand it. He trusts that I will keep showing up, keep trying.

And he's right.

I've never known lasting safety. So, even when it's offered freely—*especially* when it's offered freely—I question it.

In my past, trust was always a trick. A setup for disappointment. For betrayal.

But not with him.

When the alarm bells go off in my mind and distrust starts to scream, I almost always spiral. I get stuck in a loop, doubting the things people say.

This is especially true when it comes to compliments.

I always think, *They're just saying that to be nice.* Or, *If they knew me better, they wouldn't say those things.*

I convince myself I'm preventing pain by not allowing myself to trust others' words completely.

I can't always lean into Jason's unconditional love. Because all I can think about is how much it will hurt when it's gone.

I tell myself I'm protecting myself. That it'll hurt less if he dies. That it'll hurt less if he leaves me.

That's not true.

I know distrust is a second arrow.

It's not just how much I let Jason love me that determines how much I will hurt. It's also how much I love him.

To withhold that love feels like an injustice to all the good he brings to my life. I don't love him less to protect myself. But I do deny him the right to love me more.

I put limits on how deeply I let myself receive love. Because if I let it in fully, it makes the loss—whether real or imagined—feel like it will destroy me.

Distrust keeps me from sitting in joy. From sitting in goodness.

Good things feel so fragile. Like if I breathe wrong, they'll blow away.

When moments of fun, excitement, happiness, or bliss come, I push them away. Every single time.

I'm afraid to feel good things because I know they won't last forever. That, inevitably, the darkness will return.

Instead of allowing myself to be in the good moments, I start bracing. I start scanning the environment. Waiting for the first sign it's going to end.

When I find it—because I always do—I use it to confirm my suspicions. Proof there's no point in sitting in the good, because it just makes returning to the difficult that much harder.

I steal my own joy every single day.

This isn't to say I don't feel good feelings. I do. I just feel them at half volume.

I don't trust them to stay.

I wish I could sit with goodness and trust it more.
I think it would feel lighter. Fresher.
Like opening the windows in spring, airing out a stale house.
New light pouring in.
Shifting the way shadows fall.
Changing my perspective.

I think it would feel like warmth in the body.
A sense of peace and ease.
Like it doesn't have to be so hard.

Goodness scares me the most. That's why I distrust it.

I'm afraid of how heavy everything will feel when the light inevitably changes. Afraid that the relief will make the weight harder to carry when it returns. Afraid of being shown what *could be*—only to have it taken away again.

This is a second arrow, too—the belief that joy isn't worth it because the return to pain will be unbearable. That it's better to never open the window at all than to feel the sting of it closing.

But there are moments when the light slips in.
When the air feels fresher for just a second.

Travel almost always brings in the light.
New experiences, new people, new places.
I can feel the possibilities, the opportunities that exist
beyond my walls.

The best example I have is yoga teacher training.

I had just quit teaching. Burnt out. Desperately needing something different.

The school year ended in June. In July, I left for a month to Bali.

I knew the trip would change me. How could it not?

Loka Yoga School gave me more than I ever could have imagined.

In the months leading up to the trip, I worked with my therapist. Brittni helped me level-set my expectations. She reminded me not to put too much pressure on myself—or the experience.

I didn't go to yoga school expecting to come back healed. Or as a new person.

I went with one goal: For one month, *be Megan.*

For one month, be brave enough to let people see me.

If it didn't go well, I wouldn't have to see them again. But if it did, I'd have proof. Proof that everyday people—not just Jason, not just my close friends—strangers from around the world could find value in me.

So, I showed up as Megan.

Messy. Wounded. Brave.

Over the course of that month, I let the other students and teachers see more of me than most of my friends ever had.

And they liked what they saw.

They held me when I faced hard truths within myself. They spoke comforting words when anxiety overwhelmed me. They shared their own struggles. They held my hand during breathwork as I released deeply held trauma. They made space for me.

I allowed myself to show up. I didn't pull back. I trusted the experience. I let it unfold without expectation.

And I found my soul family.

I found people I didn't have to explain myself to. They just loved me. They saw me beyond what happened to me—and they never wavered.

This beautiful experience didn't rewrite the programming in my mind, but it did allow me to *see* the programming for what it was.

A second arrow.

Now, at least, I can see the truth:

Distrust is a paradox.

I distrust what feels good. I accept what feels bad. The bad feels normal.

But I can offer myself a choice by acknowledging the second arrow. By choosing not to fire it.

What I never realized until recently is that I could *distrust the distrust*. I had always accepted it as fact.

People are going to hurt me. I'm going to get let down—by myself, by others.

And all of that is true. Those are the first arrows. The ones I can't avoid.

But distrust? Distrust isn't fact—it's conditioning.

My abusers taught me to expect disappointment, so I trusted that expectation without question.

It's not that I don't trust myself. I do. I trust myself to distrust everything.

But I don't have to.

That's what the second arrows are teaching me.

I often wonder what my life would be like without distrust. If I could put the second arrow down for good.

If I could trust, I could allow myself to dream without fear. Without holding myself back. Without needing to stay grounded in reality.

That's the cost of distrust—

it has kept my dreams small.

Within reach. Within logic. Within certainty.

That's not how I want to dream.

I don't want to be afraid of dreaming big.

I want to feel expansive. Like I have infinite possibilities.

I want to believe that when I find my next big dream, I will trust myself to hold it.

And if I can hold it long enough, then I can start believing in it.

Shame

For a long time, I confused shame with guilt.

I treated them as though they were synonymous.

They aren't.

Guilt is about an action: *I did something bad.*

Shame is about a person: *I am bad.*

For me, guilt isn't just a feeling. It's a tool. A weapon I use against myself. As though I'm trying to scratch the itch of shame within.

Guilt is the proof that shame demands.

Shame whispers, *You are bad.*

Guilt answers, *Here's the evidence.*

When no one believed me after I told them what my *brother* did, I felt wrong for existing. *Something must be wrong with me if I'm not worth fighting for.*

My parents shut me down for even bringing it up. I wasn't even worth a conversation.

That feeling was only reinforced by my ex-husband's abuse.

I saw only one logical conclusion:

In every situation, I am the common denominator.

I am the problem.

I am the flaw.

Shame took what was done to me and twisted it into something I believed I did to myself. Even though I *know* I didn't do anything wrong, I still think it's my fault.

Shame shows up in everything.

Anytime someone is upset, I think it's my fault.

I always think I should do more. Be more.

And then maybe—just maybe—people wouldn't be upset.

I can take any situation and ultimately tell you how it's my fault. All the time, I accept responsibility for problems I didn't create.

My shame tells me that if I can make people feel less guilty by taking on their responsibilities, then maybe, one day, I will finally be a good person.

Until then, the good people around me don't have to feel bad.

So, I absorb their responsibilities. The weight of their choices. Like I'm a sponge that was built for it.

Like it's the only way I know to expand.

So, why not let it go?

Why not put down the second arrow?

Because I don't always recognize it.

Shame makes my internal dialogue make sense. If everyone else sees me as the problem, then the monster in my mind—the one telling me I am worthless—is only doing what it's supposed to.

Shame makes the monster in my mind make sense.

Shame feels like protection.

If I believe I'm inherently bad and broken, I can keep my heart safe. I can prepare myself for when someone else says the same. It won't hurt as much—because it's only confirming what I already know.

I don't know how to exist without carrying blame. It feels like my role.

Putting this second arrow down terrifies me because I don't know who I am without it.

Shame has been a constant companion. A well-worn pair of shoes. A child's favorite stuffed animal.

I don't go anywhere without it.

I carry shame so others don't have to. If they can hold the light, I'll take the darkness.

I know how to hold that.

I sound altruistic, but I'm not. Shame is the mechanism I use to keep myself from feeling goodness.

I tell myself I don't deserve it. I tell myself I'll break it. That I'll ruin it for others.

Shame is my tool to keep me from feeling what I'm least comfortable with.

In many ways, I see shame as a protector. One that weighs me down. One that whispers, over and over, all the ways I am wrong.

Not good.

Broken.

It's my darkest second arrow. One I grab easily. One I fire at will.

It's also one I don't know how to survive without.

Shame has held on so tightly because it has convinced me that I need it. Without it, I'll be vulnerable. Unprepared. Dangerously open to disappointment.

Sometimes shame screams through a megaphone. Sometimes it whispers.

But it's *always* there.

When things feel too good, too relaxed, shame grows louder. It makes its presence impossible to ignore.

I can't ever really set it down. At least, not yet.

But when I recognize that I'm shooting myself with a second arrow, I can make the choice to stop. To ignore its voice.

And I've learned something about shame—

it can't coexist with vulnerability.

When I allow myself to take up space, to be seen, fully—that's when shame is the quietest.

It's not speechless. But it definitely has less to say.

When I'm fully seen, there's nothing left for shame to distort.

When shame loses its grip, I don't just feel lighter. I feel real.

Shame kept me hidden. But I'm *here* now.

Sharing my story is my "fuck you" to shame.

I know it won't go away. I know I can't erase it.

But owning my story means shame doesn't control the narrative anymore.

I do.

Maybe I can't relax into the good just yet—but I can relax into *knowing* it's coming.

That I've created space for it.

I'm finally starting to put this second arrow down.

Control

This is my sneakiest second arrow.

Not because I enjoy it—but because I often don't even *see* it as a second arrow.

Control feels like steadiness in the body, so the absence of it feels wobbly. Like I can't get my footing.

Like scrambling up the side of a hill with nothing to grip. No ledges to hold my weight. One wrong step away from free falling.

A lack of control creates an immediate wave of anxiety.

My breath turns shallow. It speeds up. I feel my heartbeat in my gut. Sometimes I can even *see* it—pulsing, throbbing beneath my skin.

My body tenses. Claustrophobia sets in. Like the entire world is closing in. Like I won't be able to break free.

It's like my body knows before my mind does that control is slipping—and it freaks the fuck out.

Thoughts swirl too fast to separate, catching bits and pieces of static, but never the full message. Which only adds to the anxiety.

I immediately start planning for worst-case scenarios. My thinking turns negative. My energy shifts. Optimism and hope feel impossible to find.

Feeling out of control makes me hyper-focused. I spiral. My mind takes me down the darkest rabbit holes it can find.

That's why control has always felt like safety to me.

Since I was a little kid. Little Me.

If I knew what to anticipate. I could plan for it. I wouldn't be taken by surprise. Caught off guard.

Control is predictability.

If I know *what's* going to happen and *how* it's going to happen, then I know my plans will work. I know I'll be safe.

No matter which plan it is.

If I can predict how events will unfold, I can predict the safest outcome.

So much of this was learned from my childhood with Joy.

She held me, and the entire family, responsible for keeping her emotions in check.

We needed to predict what she would do. How she might act. And plan our actions accordingly.

That's what kept me safe from her.

It was impossible to control everything, all the time.

Inevitably, she would blow up. Or hit me. Or withhold love as punishment.

Some moments, I knew I needed better plans. More control.

So, I tried to find it.

Even in the things that were never mine to control.

When something didn't go as planned, I blamed myself. *I failed.* I didn't predict well enough. I would learn for next time.

I wasn't just trying to control outcomes—I was trying to control danger.

If I could predict it, maybe I could stop it.

Even now, control keeps me in a cycle of anxiety. An engine idling, never running out of gas, anxiety hums in the background.

I'm always looking for more ways to find control. Often getting stuck when I can't. Unable to move forward. Convinced there's something more I *should* be doing.

But control doesn't calm anxiety—it fuels it.

What I think will save me only keeps me stuck.

The loss of control isn't just uncomfortable—it's panic-inducing.

Full-scale, hyperventilating panic attacks. The kind that make me panic about *panicking.*

Control isn't just a preference—it's a need.

Losing it doesn't just feel unsettling—it feels like a full-body threat.

I've built my entire life around control, or at least the illusion of it.

But my healing work led me to mindfulness.

And mindfulness pulled back the curtain.

I started noticing all the small ways I was grasping. Reaching for anything to help me feel safe.

The stories I created in my mind—to make myself feel better. Or worse.

I started to see control for what it really was:

A false sense of safety.

Yes, some things are within my control. But nowhere near as much as I thought.

I can't control the opinions of others. Or the past. The future. Whether I'm misunderstood. How things will turn out.

When I started noticing this, I also started noticing the things I do internally: The way I shuffle my needs. Bury my desires. All in the name of protecting control. Offsetting the actions of others.

I've learned that control and shame are deeply intertwined for me.

I absorb the responsibilities of others because it gives me control.

If something isn't *their* problem, it becomes *mine*.

Which means I get to control it. Which means I feel safer.

Much like shame, control is about protection. But it's also about masking fear.

The fear of not being enough. Of being too much. Being rejected. Abandoned. Unloved. Unworthy.

All of it.

I don't cling to control because I want power. I cling to control because I'm afraid of what happens without it.

This is where the parable from the Buddha changed everything for me.

At any given moment, I'm having anxious thoughts. Guaranteed.

Knowingly or unknowingly.

But sometimes I recognize them. I can see the story forming in my mind—a story designed to scare me into making plans. To push me toward control.

When I can see my anxiety and my need for control for what they really are—*a self-sustained lie*—I can put the arrow back in its quiver.

Seconds later, I'll reach for it again.

And maybe I'll fire it.

Maybe I won't.

But that's how I know healing is working.

Because before, I didn't know I *could* choose.

Healing isn't about never picking up the arrow again. It's about re-membering you can set it down.

Now, I regularly ask myself, *Is this a second arrow?*

That one question has helped me understand so much.

It's helped me see how I contribute to my own suffering. How control isn't just something I grip—it's something I've learned to question.

And when I catch that moment—the moment where I choose whether to fire the second arrow or not—I almost always put it down.

Not because I believe I deserve goodness. Not because I trust events to unfold in a way that will keep me safe.

But because I've decided—I'm already suffering enough.

I don't need to suffer even more.

Fear of Success

Jesus Christ.

I am so messy.

I mean, why the fuck should success be scary?

Isn't that what *everyone* wants?

The thought of it all going right?

I feel that fear in my body. A nervous tension in my stomach—butter-flies mixed with nausea.

There's this pull inside me, like my insides want to squeal in delight. I'm excited. But I'm also terrified.

There's big shit on the line. I can feel the pressure. To do right by everyone. To do right by me.

That's what scares me most—letting myself down.

I'm afraid it might hurt more than any other hurt I've ever known.

Because letting myself down now means being disappointed in some-one I'm starting to like.

What a weird fucking feeling.

Before, I didn't care about making *me* happy. I cared about being liked. Keeping others calm because it kept me calm.

Now, it's different. Now, I want to make sure every past version of me is proud.

If I know I didn't do my best, it means the monster in my mind will know too.

If it knows, it means I will have a reason to mercilessly bully myself.

I can hate myself with purpose. Fueled by the proof of my failures.

I'm worried about moving in the wrong direction. I'm worried about stumbling backward in my healing.

I've worked hard to make space for *big* dreams.

I don't want to fuck it all up.

Success is scarier now because I'm finally doing what I care about. Not what I think will make other people happy.

I get to have bigger dreams—but that means bigger risks.

The fear of success paralyzes me, just thinking about it.

Now, *I* matter in the equation. Now, my dreams are on the line.

This is where perfectionism fucking sucks.

"My best" is an unrealistic standard. Something I cannot reach.

I *know* this.

But I strive for it anyway.

Like a compulsion.

That's the mindfuck of perfectionism.

I *know* I can't get there.

Every single task is doomed to fail before it begins.

But I keep trying—because pain and struggle are all I know.

Struggle has been my constant companion. My proof of worthiness.

If an accomplishment didn't hurt, didn't require suffering—then how could it possibly matter? How could it be real?

This is a second arrow.

My story *did* hurt. It *did* require suffering.

Not in the telling of it—but in living it.

The struggle already happened. I survived the hard part.

But if something comes with ease, I worry I've done something wrong.

That there's a trick. That I'm a fraud.

In my mind, ease means failure. And struggle means worthiness.

If something comes naturally—if it flows—it feels suspect.

I must have missed something. I must not be doing enough.

But growth doesn't have to be fueled by suffering. It can also be fueled by ease.

I've been afraid to share my story. Hiding from it my entire life.

Worried I couldn't get out of my mind and body enough to share.

Worried I *could.*

Worried I wouldn't know what to say.

I don't know who I am without the chase. Without the pressure. Without the fear.

I asked Brittni about it.

"If I don't have the anxious energy driving me…
If I don't have the need to prove myself fueling me…
If I don't have the voice telling me to be better, faster, stronger…
What happens to me?
Without those things, will I stop?
Will the engine die?"

Brittni pointed out that maybe that's the point.

I get to find out.
If I can feel both excitement and fear at the same time,
maybe I don't have to silence one to make room for the other.
Maybe they can exist together.
Maybe that's what it means to be brave.
To take chances.
To feel fully alive.

But how do I even learn to relax into possibility?

It sounds lovely. Like a playground for the mind. A beauty that sends warmth through my body.

But then I think of all the possible dangers. The failures. The disappointments.

I get consumed by them.

I feel the tickle of dread in my spine. Deep within. A shiver of doubt.

It whispers, *What if I mess it up? What if I ruin this beauty?*

My fear of success often disguises itself as preparation. It tells me it's keeping me safe. It's keeping me ready. It's the only thing standing between me and total disaster.

But now I'm starting to wonder—

What if the beauty isn't as fragile as I think?
What if it's not something I have to hold perfectly?
What if it can hold me?

Possibility isn't just a door to failure.
It's a door to the unimaginable.

Bigger, wilder, more expansive than my fear
allows me to see.

Maybe success isn't the absence of fear.
Maybe success is moving forward
even when fear is clawing at my throat.

Maybe success is knowing fear will always be there—
and doing it anyway.

Maybe success is asking different questions.

What if I don't ruin it?
What if I rise to meet it?
What if I'm already becoming
the version of myself who knows how to hold it?

Relaxing into possibility isn't about silencing the fear.
It's about learning to let it be
there without letting it take the wheel.

The doubt will whisper.
The fear will creep in.
The shiver will run down my spine.

But I don't have to follow it.

I can notice it.
Acknowledge it.
And still choose to step forward anyway.

I can do it scared.

Surviving was scary.
Healing is scary.
Success is scary.

Most days, I feel so weak.
I'm afraid of my own shadow.

I've faced it all.
Survived it all.
Shared it all.

But I'm still fucking scared.

I still feel so fucking small.

I know life isn't easy.
I know good things don't come without risk.

But fuck—just once, I want to feel like I can move
forward without being afraid.

It's so unfair.

And I am just so goddamn tired.

Tired of having to be brave.
Tired of pushing through.
Tired of feeling like goodness must be earned—

with another layer of fear.
Another mountain to climb.
Another moment of white-knuckling my way through.

If that's all healing can ever offer me—
the opportunity to suffer less—
then it's fucking worth it.

I've been to the edge of deep suffering.
And I have no intention of going back.

Healing is helping me put down the second arrows—
before I bleed out from the wounds.

I will still reach for the arrows.
But now, I know—

I don't have to take the shot.

13.

Maps, Medicines, and Messes

Healing doesn't follow a formula. It's highly personal, deeply contextual, and sometimes downright weird. And it didn't arrive all at once. It came in layers. In fragments. In pieces I collected slowly over time, like driftwood from a shipwreck I was still trying to understand.

I've spent a lot of time, energy, and money trying to understand myself. That is a privilege. And I don't want to pretend otherwise.

Access to healing isn't equitable.

Not everyone has the space, the resources, the time, or the support to go looking for what might help.

So much of what I've found has come not just through effort—but through access. And I carry that awareness with me, even as I reflect on what helped.

I've been fortunate enough to try a wide variety of tools. Some opened doors I'd spent decades keeping locked. Some cracked things open before I felt ready. And others—honestly—just didn't land.

But over time, I found a few that helped me come back to myself. Not in grand, transformative bursts—but in small, barely-noticed ways. A breath. A pause. A flicker of sensation in a body I'd long stopped calling home.

Beneath all the trying—beneath the impulse to fix myself fast—was something truer: a quiet, persistent need to understand why I hurt the way I did. Why I disappeared. Why I couldn't stay with myself.

I didn't know I was gathering a language. I didn't know I was building a map. But I was.

These tools didn't save me. But they are helping me come back for myself, piece by piece.

Yoga and Trauma-Sensitive Yoga

One of the first tools that found me—long before I understood what I was healing—was yoga.

I started practicing over fifteen years ago, shortly after leaving my abusive ex-husband.

At the time, I wasn't looking for healing. I was just looking for a workout that wouldn't overwhelm me.

I've never been comfortable in gyms, but I was flexible, and yoga felt accessible.

I didn't have the mental bandwidth for a steep learning curve—I just wanted something I could do. Something that gave me a reason to move.

From the beginning, I loved being on my mat.

I loved the paradox of it—being in a room full of people, but having a space that was entirely my own. No one would enter it. No one could ask anything of me while I was there.

For sixty minutes, I wasn't trying to survive—I was just breathing. Just moving.

For almost a decade, I practiced the way I lived: rigidly.

I followed the teacher's instructions to the letter, even if I was tired, sore, or on the verge of collapse.

I wouldn't take child's pose. I wouldn't skip a vinyasa.

I believed permission had to come from outside of me—and if I didn't earn it, I didn't deserve rest.

I judged people who did less. But they weren't doing less. They were doing what I hadn't yet learned to do.

They were listening to their bodies. I was performing with mine.

They were practicing yoga. I was performing pain.

Eventually—between all the poses I forced and the breath I ignored—I started hearing things.

A quiet voice beneath the teacher's cues. A gentle nudge to soften.

I began to notice when my body whispered, *No.*

I started googling the philosophy of yoga. The other limbs beyond asana, or the physical practice. And what I found stopped me cold.

It wasn't about achieving poses. Yoga was about coming home.

I fell in love with the deeper layers—*pratyahara* (withdrawing the senses), *pranayama* (breath), *dhyana* (meditation).

These practices didn't ask me to perform. They asked me to feel. To stay. To notice when I left myself—and to come back without punishment.

Yoga gave me a way back into my body when I wasn't sure I wanted one.

I still float away. Every single day, I forget I have a body. I live in my head. I plan, I analyze, I brace.

But yoga has given me the ability to notice it sooner—and return more gently.

That's why it's called a practice. Not a performance. Not a product. Not a perfection.

A *practice.*

In 2023, I went to Bali to become a yoga teacher.

I didn't know it then, but it changed my life.

I'd already been undergoing what I can only describe as a spiritual unraveling.

I felt a growing hunger for something I couldn't name.

I was a wife, a mother, a sister, a friend—but I needed something that belonged to *me*. Something that made me feel alive again. Not numb. Not armored.

While I was there, one of my teachers told me she thought I was a natural. That teaching was my dharma, my life's calling.

I came home and started teaching yoga immediately. And I loved it. I thought maybe I had found my purpose.

But not long after, my depression deepened. My own practice began to fade. I only unrolled my mat to teach others.

I felt like I was failing—at yoga, at purpose, at staying connected. I knew I was close to something that mattered, but I also knew I wasn't quite there.

And the fog of depression was getting thicker. Making everything harder to see. To feel. To trust.

And then I remembered a trauma-sensitive yoga class I'd taken years earlier.

And I knew I found my missing piece. I just didn't know what to do with it.

In 2024, despite my depression, I signed up for a six-month trauma-sensitive yoga teacher training.

In that training, I learned how trauma lives in the body—not just as pain, but as absence.

How it rewired my brain to protect me by cutting off access to memory, especially the good ones.

How it shut down my ability to feel my body from the inside.

That embodiment wasn't just something I'd lost—it was something I'd never really had.

Maybe most importantly, I learned it's not gone forever.

It just has to be gently, patiently, relearned.

I started practicing presence not as a performance, but as a kindness.

I began to feel small flickers of sensation return—my feet on the floor, my breath when I didn't force it, the ache behind my sternum when I softened for even a moment.

Embodiment became less about being in my body all the time and more about noticing when I'd left. And then returning. Over and over again. Without shame.

That's why I chose to become an embodiment coach.

Not because I have it mastered.

But because I know what it means to be numb.

To disappear into my mind.

To live an entire life disconnected from the only home I'll ever really have.

And I know the quiet miracle of coming back.

Yoga was never the whole answer.

But it was the first place I stopped running—and the first place I started listening.

Mindfulness

Mindfulness was not easy for me.

Stillness wasn't a comfort—it was a confrontation.

Early on, every time I tried to sit in silence, my mind would spiral.

I'd remember things I needed to do.

Replay conversations from twenty years ago.

Ponder a random fact about Iceland I learned when I was ten.

Plan the weekend.

Get a song stuck on loop.

My body would feel restless and my chest would tighten.

I thought that meant I was doing it wrong.

I thought mindfulness was supposed to be peaceful.

Like I was supposed to be so deep within myself that nothing could break my focus.

I thought being present meant being calm. And calm meant being still. And still meant silent. And silent meant successful.

So I'd sit on my meditation cushion, feeling like a failure.

Shaming myself for not being able to listen. To pause. To be still. To be calm—whatever the fuck that meant.

My ADHD and my meditation practice were at odds.

It was like my attention was a caged animal, and the second I closed my eyes, it would start pacing. Clawing. Growling to be let out. And sometimes, I'd let it.

Other times, I'd white-knuckle my way through the practice and call it discipline. But really it was just endurance.

It took me a long time to realize that calm doesn't mean the same thing for everyone.

And even longer to realize that presence doesn't require calm at all.

For me, calm doesn't always mean quiet. It doesn't look like deep stillness or a blank mind or a softly glowing room.

Sometimes it looks like movement. Or fidgeting. Or walking in circles while repeating a grounding phrase under my breath.

Sometimes calm is just the moment I resist the urge to judge myself for not being calm.

That's what mindfulness taught me.

Not how to quiet my mind, but how to be with it.

To notice the chaos without becoming it. To feel the discomfort and stay anyway.

Even after two Mindful-Based Stress Reduction (MBSR) classes, I could only do it for a few seconds at a time. Then a few minutes.

Now, after years of practice—and becoming a mindfulness teacher— I can sometimes stay a little longer in the moment.

I still can't sit cross-legged for long without needing to shift or adjust my body, and I don't always remember to breathe deeply.

But when I can be present with myself, sometimes things shift.
I remember I don't have to react to every thought. I can watch them rise. Let them pass. And know they will likely come back around again.

I don't always get it right. Some days I still get distracted.
But mindfulness gives me the grace to come back. Not with force. Not with shame. Just with breath.

It lets me witness my life in the only place it's actually happening— right now.

Not in the memories I keep reliving.

Not in the imagined disasters I try to prevent.

But here. In this moment.

And this one.

And this one.

It's also helped me start to untangle my past from my present. To recognize that I'm not reliving those old moments—my nervous system just hasn't caught up yet because it's still learning what safety looks like.

Mindfulness gives me just enough space to notice: this isn't then. And when I can catch that truth in real time, I get to choose how I respond.

I don't have to repeat old patterns. I don't have to disappear. I can stay. I can live my life as it's unfolding.

Even the boring parts. Even the ones I used to miss because I was bracing for the next thing.

I don't have to wait for a moment to become a memory so I can feel safe living inside it.

Mindfulness didn't make the pain disappear. It just helped me stop time traveling long enough to notice I was still alive.

And that noticing—that witnessing—is its own kind of miracle.

Ketamine Therapy

Before I ever tried ketamine, I spent over five years on Lexapro.

I was told it would help with my anxiety. That it might take the edge off the depression. That I'd start to feel a little more like myself.

But I never really did.

It didn't make anything worse. But it didn't make anything better either.

I still felt the same waves of sadness. The same gripping anxiety. The same detachment from my body, from joy, from myself.

The only time I noticed it was doing something was when I forgot to take it.

Then came the brain zaps—weird little shocks that felt like electricity behind my eyes or static in my skull.

They were disorienting and frequent. A literal mental cue that I forgot my medicine.

They were the only evidence I had that Lexapro was in my system at all.

I stayed on it for years because I thought maybe it was working in some invisible way I just wasn't grateful enough to notice. That I was too detached from my body for it to register.

Or maybe I was the problem. Maybe I just needed to try harder, or wait longer, or accept that this muted version of life was as good as it was going to get.

But eventually, I realized I wasn't feeling anything.

Not worse. Not better. Just flat.

TikTok taught me I wasn't alone. That a lot of people struggle with finding the right antidepressant and many never will due to treatment resistance. I was stuck.

The only option my general practitioner could give was to take the long road of weaning off of one antidepressant before slowly starting another one.

It could take years to find the right one, and all the while my symptoms would persist.

Lexapro didn't bring me home to myself.

It didn't quiet my mind or lift the heaviness in my chest.

It didn't give me access to the parts of me that were shut down—it just made them easier to ignore.

So I came off it. Slowly. Carefully.

I went back to navigating my own mind with nothing to hold on to.

It was like I was on a carnival ride with no safety bar.

Sure, the Lexapro didn't help, but at least it was there.

Almost a year after I quit Lexapro, my therapist, Brittni, suggested ketamine therapy.

I stalled out in talk therapy. Frustrated because I couldn't move forward despite her or my best efforts.

Brittni said ketamine has been shown to help people who feel stuck— even when they've tried everything else.

People like me.

She wasn't promising miracles. Just possibility.

A different kind of access point. One that didn't require words or memory or perfectly constructed narratives.

She said it might help me loosen the grip trauma had on my body. On my mind. On my life.

At first, I hesitated.

The idea of a psychedelic felt like too much. Too uncontained. Too unknown.

But the truth was, I didn't feel contained in myself anyway. I was already living half-alive.

So I said yes.

I didn't know what to expect from ketamine therapy.

I just knew I was running out of ways to access what I couldn't reach.

I was doing the work—talk therapy, embodiment, mindfulness, journaling—but there were still rooms inside me I couldn't unlock. Parts of me I couldn't even find.

Jason and Brittni went with me to my first session.

We spoke with the doctors. We listened as one told us about his own revelatory experience on ketamine in the hospital.

He told us about patients unlocking old memories. Forgiving themselves for old hurts. Finding a way to come to peace with their pasts.

It felt incredibly hopeful. And a little too good to be true.

I was nervous when they started my IV.

My anxiety spiked my blood pressure, so they gave me something to bring it down. They also gave me something in case I experienced any nausea.

Then they started the ketamine.

My first dose was light. I don't remember much about the experience, just that it was pleasant and that Jason kept me company.

I had a session immediately afterwards with Brittni, which is the ideal way to use the tool.

Ketamine's magic lies in that your brain is highly neuroplastic for 24-48 hours after the treatment, so it's easier to rewire stuck patterns and limiting beliefs. To reframe old stories and wounds.

It's not to make the trauma go away, but to change your relationship with it.

To not let the past continue to control the present.

It's a great time to meet with a therapist. To talk about challenges and accelerate recovery.

I felt incredible after the first ketamine session. Almost giddy. I was smiling. Brittni was happy, too. We could both tell this was going to be something.

I completed six sessions in three weeks while we found the right dosage.

From there, I started going once a month for maintenance. Then every six weeks. Now, I go every eight weeks.

My sessions are different every time.

I wish I could say I had one of the deep healing experiences on ketamine, but I mostly just see colors and feel connected to the oneness of things.

I leave my body. I leave my thoughts. And for forty-five minutes or so, I float in peace.

So, how do I know it's doing anything?

Because since starting ketamine, I get out of my own way easier.

I can see it in my thinking. I'm not as quick to make judgments. I look for the lessons.

I can feel it in how I talk to myself. I'm kinder and give myself a little more space to make a mistake.

Every time I talk to myself differently, it sends a spark to my stomach.

One that gets my attention.

One that says, *"Look what you just did."*

It's a spark of pride. Of proof.

I wasn't looking for a miracle. I was looking for *a crack.*

Ketamine gave me that.

What surfaced after starting ketamine surprised me.

I didn't just see what had been done to me—I saw what I had done to myself.

It wasn't a dramatic moment. It was quiet. Almost *tender.*

And I didn't feel hatred or judgment.

I felt grief.

Grief for the girl who felt disposable. Who wasn't believed. Who carried it all alone.

Grief for the woman who thought disappearing would keep her safe. Who believed the comfort of others was more important than her own.

I saw her. And I didn't look away. I stayed.

That's what ketamine gave me: space for the work I was doing with Brittni to stick. Space to witness the whole story.

Not just the pain, but the part I played in keeping it alive. Not with cruelty. But with compassion. With context.

I'm not done with ketamine. I don't know when I will be.

I don't feel "cured." I feel more open. I feel like I dropped a stone into the deepest well of myself—and it finally touched bottom.

And that's where the real work finally had space to begin.

Not because ketamine fixed me. But because it finally let me feel the part of me that still wanted to be found.

EMDR

I put off EMDR for a long time. It scared me. Not because I didn't think it would work—but because I *did*.

Because I knew there were things in the recesses of my mind I hadn't let myself remember. Things tucked in the gaps. The moments that don't appear in flashbacks, but still dictate how I live.

I was terrified of what might surface. Terrified I wouldn't be able to handle it if it did.

It felt like conducting a post mortem on my memory—but without knowing what I'd find, or how bad it might be.

What if I uncovered more trauma?

More gaps in my memory?

More failures?

More reasons to blame myself?

But Brittni thought I was ready. She thought I could handle it.

She said I wouldn't be doing it alone.

She'd be there, and I was adding Morgan to my team, too.

So I said yes.

And it has been, hands down, the bravest work I've ever done.

EMDR doesn't feel like talk therapy.

It's not a conversation. It's not about explaining or justifying.

It's more like being led into a memory you didn't realize was still alive—and then being given a chance to *change how it lives inside you.*

I sit, cross my arms on my chest, and alternate tapping my hands on my shoulders.

The bilateral stimulation allows the brain to process memories without the same level of emotional connection I might have in talk therapy.

Sometimes, it brings up images I haven't seen in decades.
Sometimes, it's body sensations with no story attached.
Sometimes, it's just blankness—and even that holds something.
Even the blanks are part of the pattern. *My pattern.*

My mind bounces between thoughts and memories. Many are painful.

Grief for having to take care of myself as a child. For not being protected. For when no one noticed I was barely keeping it together.

Sometimes I ugly cry. Snot comes out of my nose. My eyes become red and puffy.

EMDR acts as a pressure valve.

It's a way to bring the big emotions, the ones I buried deep, to the surface, without setting off my body's alarm systems.

Each session is a challenge. I still get anxious.

I still wonder if I'm going to hit something too big for me to handle. Something too sharp. Too buried. Or find proof I was the problem all along.

But I keep going, because it's *working.*

EMDR has helped me access the negative core beliefs that have shaped my entire life—some I didn't even know I was carrying.

But what matters is that I'm finally *seeing them.* Naming them. And, slowly, with Morgan and Brittni's help, I'm reframing them.

Not in a fake, "positive affirmations" kind of way. In a way that *lands.* That sticks. That gives me choice.

Like maybe my mother's lack of protection had nothing to do with me.
Maybe it wasn't my fault.
Maybe it's not my guilt to carry.

Maybe justice isn't about punishment or apology.
Maybe it's about refusing to harden my heart.
Maybe it's about putting down the armor.
Not in defeat.
But in protest.

The truth is, EMDR still scares me.

But I would do it a million times over. Because it's not just helping me understand myself—it's helping me *change.*

And for the first time, that change feels like it's coming from the inside.

Not because someone told me what to believe.
Not because I'm trying to please or perform.
Not because I believe I will be loved if I do.

But because I want the change. Because it's who I've been all along. And it's who I am becoming.

EMDR has helped me see things I didn't want to.

Things that were living beneath my shame and silence.

Things I had spent years running from because I thought naming them would make them true.

Because if I said them out loud, maybe I *would* be bad. Maybe I'd lose everything. Maybe I'd deserve to.

But now they're rising.

And I'm learning how to hold them.

14.

The Armor and the Ache

Working on healing helped to give shape to parts of my story, yes—but it also exposed what had been living underneath it all along.

Things I didn't fully understand until I began to slow down.

Until I stopped bracing.

Until I sat in the silence long enough for something deeper to surface.

It's easy to think healing will feel like closure. Like catharsis. Like what will lead you to feeling "normal."

And sometimes, it does. But for me, it's also doing something else.

It made space for something more honest. More terrifying. More sacred.

Healing didn't close the wounds—it cleared the debris.

And the real reckoning didn't come during therapy or yoga or any particular moment. It came after.

In the quiet. In the spaces I'd spent my life avoiding.

These are the truths I didn't see coming.

The ones I've been circling my whole life. And now, finally, they've found their way to the surface.

They are new. They are raw. I'm still making sense of them.

Anti-Hero

I have always secretly believed I might be a bad person.

I've been collecting good behaviors like receipts, offering them to the universe as proof that I deserve to be here. That I deserve to be alive.

This one belief has quietly shaped everything.
Every choice. Every relationship. Every moment of hesitation.

It's why I've worried Jason would realize he's too good for me.

That I expect everyone to leave me, so I leave them first.

That I think if people only knew me better, they'd see the truth.

It's like there's a kernel of something that I can't name and can't locate, but it worries me. I've used it to explain everything that's happened to me.

I've spent half my life not being believed. Not being protected.

Instead I was blamed. I was hurt. I was violated.

For a long time, I thought that's just how people loved me.

I was the common denominator in all of my pain, so maybe there's something wrong with me.

Some flaw I can't see or fix, but it's something others can pick up on.

EMDR is helping me understand this is how younger versions of me grasped for control when they felt powerless. But that doesn't make it true.

Little Me and Teen Me didn't have the capacity to process that the adults who were supposed to protect them had failed.

Instead, they blamed themselves.

They believed it was all their fault.

That if they could have just been better, been "good," they never would have been hurt.

I've carried that story my entire life.

I'm working on trying to believe I'm a good person. And the proof I have is that I didn't hurt other people. Even when I could have.

What if it's not compassion?

What if it's overcompensation?

What if it's just a stage rehearsal for goodness—while I keep hiding the villain I'm terrified might actually be me?

The grief is almost unbearable because I can see just how much I've lost to this belief.

How much of me was shaped around the fear of being bad.

It's insidious. It's in everything.

It's in the way I can't accept compliments.

How I deflect them. Diminish them. Twist them into something untrue.

Not because I'm being modest—but because I genuinely don't think I deserve them.

It's in the way I downplay my accomplishments.

Not to be humble.

But because I don't believe I should be celebrated. Because celebration feels fraudulent. Like I've tricked someone into thinking I'm better than I am.

I don't feel pride when I accomplish something. I feel relief.

Relief that it's over. That I didn't fail. That I didn't let anyone down. That I collected another receipt for the universe to prove I deserve to keep existing.

Every good deed. Every kind word. Every check mark on my to-do list—
all of it gets filed away as evidence.

Not of who I am. But of who I'm *trying* to be.

Of who I need the world to believe I am so they don't see the truth I still believe lives underneath it all.

A fraud.
A liability.
A bad person in a good person costume.

That's the hardest part.

It doesn't matter how many people love me, or believe in me, or tell me otherwise—
because there's a part of me that still wonders if they've all just been fooled.

That's the part EMDR is helping me meet.

Not to silence her. But to understand her.

To learn where she came from. And what she's still trying to protect me from.

I've spent my life living and breathing for the external validation of others—because I needed proof of goodness for myself.

My perfectionism wasn't about ambition.

It was a defense. A disguise. A lifeline.

If I could turn in something that was flawless—something that exceeded expectations, that earned praise, that stunned—maybe I'd have proof.

Proof that I wasn't bad.

That I wasn't stupid. Or lazy. Or unworthy of existing at all.

I have two undergraduate degrees, a master's, and everything for a doctorate but the dissertation. I'm a National Board Certified teacher.

I hold four additional certifications in education. I'm a certified project manager.

I'm not trying to brag. I didn't even want most of these things.

But achievement became my language of survival.

My shield. My currency.

I don't look at any of these diplomas or certifications with pride.

I look at them as evidence from an ongoing crime scene of self-erasure.

If I could just keep stacking up credentials—stacking up evidence— maybe I could silence the voice in my head that kept whispering: *You're not enough. You're a fraud. They're going to find out.*

Rest wasn't neutral. It was dangerous.

So I didn't relax. I produced. I performed.

Because survival, in my mind, depended on output.

And it hasn't just been in academics or work.

I accept blame for other people's mistakes because I'd rather be seen as wrong than risk making someone else feel ashamed.

When someone hurts me, I don't speak up.

I tell them it's okay. I tell them I understand. I comfort them.

Because I'd rather feel pain than cause someone else to.

I've let people walk all over me just so they wouldn't feel uncomfortable.

I've stayed quiet when I knew the right answer—because I wanted someone else to have the win.

I'm not trying to be a martyr here.

I didn't do these things to be kind, though it may have come off that way.

I did them to be *safe*.

That's how deeply I believed being good was the only way I would be allowed to exist.

And now, I'm grieving her, too. The version of me who thought self-destruction was the only way to stay good.

The one who turned herself inside out trying to earn what should have been unconditional.

I'm still trying to learn how to receive what doesn't have a price.

Still trying to believe I was never bad—just afraid. Just surviving.

Just shaped by a world that taught me love had to be earned.

That worth was a transaction.

But maybe that was all a lie I told myself a long time ago.

Maybe being a person is enough.

The One I Forgot to Include

The second lifelong belief is harder to hold.

Because it's not just painful—it's humiliating.

I've been hurting someone my entire life.

And that someone is me.

But it wasn't the kind of harm that showed up in bruises.

It was the kind that sounded like truth.

I said things to myself no one else had to say. Because I got there first.

I told myself I was lazy. Selfish. Manipulative. Stupid.

I called myself a disappointment so no one else had to.

I critiqued my body, my face, my voice, my ideas.

Nothing was ever good enough.

I was never good enough.

Not because I believed I caused all the harm in my life.

But because I believed I *deserved* all of the punishment.

It was like I'd internalized this unspoken rule: If I suffered enough, it would somehow balance the scales.

Like pain could make me pure.

Like if I could just *hurt enough*, I might finally be forgiven for existing.

Or earn the right to.

So I aimed for record speed.

I punished myself for every mistake, every misstep, every imagined flaw.

Every time I forgot something. Or dreamed too big.

Every should've, would've, could've became another link in the chain I dragged behind me.

Honestly, I think I was training for the Suffering Olympics. And I was determined to take gold.

I was Jacob—or maybe Robert—Marley in *A Christmas Carol* (shout-out to the Muppet version).

Except I wasn't dead.

I was walking through my life *alive* and still bound to the chains of shame, guilt, self-loathing, and self-abandonment I'd forged link by link.

The worst part?

I thought this made me good.

I thought this *proved* I wasn't like the ones who hurt me.

That if I could hate myself hard enough, I'd be safe.

That if I got there first, I'd beat the world to the punch.

I didn't realize the punches were already landing. Because I was the one throwing them.

How do I reconcile *that* with the fear of being a bad person?

Talk about a mindfuck.

How can I be a good person if I've spent a lifetime waging war against myself?

How can I be a good person and treat myself with unspeakable cruelty?

My values would say I can't.

That harming another person the way I harmed myself—by eroding my self-esteem and self-worth—would make me a bad person.

The reframe I got from EMDR is that I didn't intend to hurt myself.

I was following a script handed to me before I had language.

Self-abandonment was taught. Modeled. Inherited.

My internal dialogue was created by my parents and reinforced by my ex-husband.

Basically, I didn't stand a chance of loving myself in those conditions.

I understand it logically, but it's not in my bones yet.

Right now, I'm sitting inside the grief of having become what I swore I'd never be.

I never wanted to be like them. Like the ones who hurt me. But I was.

Maybe not fully. But enough to do damage.

And here's the part that guts me: I did it longer.

And I didn't even notice. I didn't even think to *care*.

I didn't realize I was supposed to.

Because I was never a part of the equation.

Until now.

When the Freeze Cracked Open

It happened in Rishikesh, India, while on a yoga retreat.

I was sitting along the banks of the Ganges River, waiting for Ganga Aarti to begin—a bright, colorful ceremony held at sunset.

The kind of ritual that vibrates through your whole body.

The kind that draws hundreds of people into a tight crowd, their voices rising with the priests', hands clapping, bells ringing, smoke swirling in thick spirals toward the sky.

We were there early.

The heat was still heavy.

Flies bit at my skin.

The loudspeakers echoed chants I couldn't decipher.

The crowd pressed in close.

And then, my mind hit the emergency brake.

First came the shaking.

Then the paralysis. My body locked up. I *wanted* to move—but I couldn't.

The tremors wouldn't stop. Even when I was frozen.

My breath turned shallow. My heart pounded. My hands and feet buzzed like static.

Jason told me later that he was coaching me to breathe. He kept repeating, "You're okay. Just breathe. You're okay."

But I couldn't hear him.

Everything went silent. Not just the crowd. Not just the chants.

Everything.

My thoughts stopped racing. My internal narrator went quiet.

There was no script running. No shoulds, no plans, no fear spirals.

Just blankness.

It should have felt peaceful.

But my body was in full alarm mode.

The sheer overwhelm had triggered a total system shutdown.

Not to punish me.

To *preserve* me.

To survive.

My yoga teacher saw me shaking and came to my side.

She wrapped her arms around me, and that was enough—just enough—for the paralysis to loosen.

Jason and I started making our way through the crowd.

My vision narrowed.

My legs felt like stone.

I barely made it out before collapsing.

I was hyperventilating. Disoriented. Floating inside my own body.

A nearby medic checked my pulse—said it was racing.

He told me to wait it out, let my system calm, and get away from the stimulation.

I cried the entire tuk tuk ride back to the hotel. Barely breathing. Barely thinking.

But somewhere in that spiral—underneath the shaking, the gasping, the unraveling—
something rose to the surface.

Not a thought. Not a memory. A *knowing*.

I wasn't just having a panic attack.

I was remembering where the freeze response began.

Not in my mind—but in my *body*.

It started with her. Little Me.

She had nowhere to run. No one to protect her.

Too little to fight back.

She did the only thing she could: She froze.

And she stayed frozen, because that's what kept her alive.

For the first time, I didn't just *understand* my trauma response.

I *felt* its origin. Not in words or images—but in vibration. In muscle. In breath.

It was the moment where information became *integration*.

Where the definition of freeze response became the felt reality of it.

Where that small, terrified girl finally got my full attention.

And then I thought of her. Teen Me.

The one whose freeze felt the most unbearable.

The one who desperately wanted to run but couldn't.

Who wanted to fight but was outmatched.

So she had to endure the physical and sexual abuse without escape.

And now, decades later, her survival system was still trying to protect me.

On the banks of the Ganges River, she stepped forward—not in a vision, but in sensation.

The paralysis. The racing heart. The dissociation. It was all her. All me.

How awful it must have been for her.

Was she as scared as I was at that moment?

Did she feel her body was betraying her?

Was she begging it to move but it wouldn't?

Or was she grateful to disappear?

And here's what breaks my heart the most: she didn't choose that.

Her body did.

It chose the only option it had: to freeze.

Just like mine was doing on the banks of the Ganges.

My body told the story my mind couldn't remember. And in doing so, it helped me remember *her.*

It took a couple of days for my body to feel fully normal again.

I left India and came home with a different appreciation of my body's defense system.

I still hate that I freeze.

Still hate that I can't control it. Or even notice it sometimes.

But I don't see it as betrayal anymore.

I see it as loyalty.

Because it worked so long ago, my system kept using it and I never learned another way.

I never even thought to teach it one.

But now I'm trying.

I'm trying to give my body new tools.

Trying to stay present when I want to disappear.

Trying to show myself the same care I've spent my whole life giving to others.

For a long time, when I talked about protecting people, I wasn't included in that vision.

When I said I wanted to make the world better, I never meant *for me.*

When I imagined offering safety, I imagined it for everyone else.

I left myself out of everything.

My needs. My desires. My boundaries. My humanity.

I didn't see myself as someone worth saving.

But that's starting to shift.

Not because I've suddenly mastered self-love.

Not because I've found some secret formula for healing.

But because I'm finally remembering—I am a person, too.

I am a person, too.

That sounds so simple. But saying it out loud feels like a rebellion.

Like rewriting the script I was handed before I could speak.

I am a person.

Not a project. Not a problem. Not a collection of mistakes.

A person.

And I want to include her now.

In the safety. In the softness. In the protection.

In the peace I've tried so hard to create for everyone else.

I don't always know how. But I know I want to.

And that's a start.

I began to wonder—if I'm finally including myself now, who might I become if I keep going?

15.

Forward

Future Me steps forward, giving me a moment to take her in.

This is big for me.

I think she knows it.

She knows how long I've been waiting for this moment—even if I wasn't always sure it would come.

She smiles.

"Hey, you."

I take a moment.

Breathe it all in.

I can already feel her magic. Her power. Her love.

I immediately drop my gaze.

"I'm sorry it took me so long to get here."

I hold my breath.

Worried she's going to be disappointed in me.

Future Me shakes her head, her smile soft but certain.

"You don't owe me an apology."

She moves closer.

Her presence steady.

Warm.

"You got here exactly when you were meant to.
No sooner, no later.
And I was never impatient.
I knew you'd find me."

She tilts her head, studying me. Her eyes full of knowing.

"The real question is…do you believe that yet?"

I think about her question. I want to find the right answer.

The one that would make her happy.

I start crafting a cleaned-up response.

Something better. More comfortable.

There's a familiar pressure in my chest.

I stop.

Take a deep breath.

Reset.

I decide not to tell her a sanitized version of the truth.

"I do believe it.
But it's hard to feel it.

To understand it.
I feel so small next to you."

She nods.

As if she expected that answer.

"Yeah. I get that."

She moves in more.

Closing the space between us just slightly.

"But you're not small, love. You never have been."

She exhales, her voice dipping into something softer.

"You just spent many years making yourself small.
Folding yourself up so no one would notice you.
Shrinking to fit into spaces never meant to hold you.
And now?"

She smiles. Tilts her head.

"Now you're just unfolding.
Stretching back into the shape you were always meant to be."

Future Me stops. Lets her words sit between us before asking—

"So, tell me—if you weren't afraid of taking up space,
what would you do right now?"

I sit back. Thinking about the question.

I don't have an answer.

It seems like I should.

"Honestly? I don't know.
I think I'm still trying to figure that out.

But I know I would be creating—
Art. Memories. All of it."

I let out a slow breath.

"I've just been so scared to take up space.
To be seen.
I still don't know how to exist
in spaces where I don't have to hide."

I pause.

My voice gets quieter.

"I know that's not a good answer. But I really don't know.
It's hard for me to understand it. To tap into it.
But I also know every cell in my body is longing for it."

She nods. Her smile warm with knowing.

"That is a good answer. It's the truth."

Future Me shifts slightly.

Still watching me with that steady, unshaken gaze.

"You've spent so much time surviving
that you never really had the luxury
of asking yourself what you wanted.
What you actually wanted—
not what would keep you safe,
not what would keep other people happy,
but you.*"*

She is quiet.

Letting the words settle before continuing.

"That's why it feels foreign.
Why you can't quite grab hold of it yet.
But that longing? The ache you feel?
That's me calling you forward."

She pauses.

Her voice softens even more.

"So maybe the better question isn't what you would do—
it's who you would be if you stopped
making yourself
small."

I tilt my head slightly. Waiting for her to tell me the answer.

"Do you know her yet?"

I blink. Confused.

"You mean you? Do I know you yet? Shouldn't you already know that?"

She laughs.

There's a sparkle in her eye. So much life.

"Exactly. Do you know me yet?"

She leans forward slightly. Resting her elbows on her knees.

"You've caught glimpses.
In the way you stand up for yourself a little more.
In the way you soften toward yourself on the hard days.
In the way you let yourself dream again,
even when it scares the hell out of you."

She pauses.

Her eyes searching my face.

"But do you really know me?
Or am I still just a concept?
A maybe?
A someday?"

Her voice lowers. Just a bit.

"Because I'm not a maybe.
I'm not some distant dream you'll never reach.
I am you.
You just haven't stepped fully into me yet."

She sits back, a knowing smirk tugging at her lips.

"So, tell me, do you know me yet?"

I look at her.

She's so much more than I could have imagined.

I start squirming in my seat. Fidgeting with my sweatshirt. Nervous to get it wrong.

"I know parts of you," I say, then hesitate. I want to stop there, but that wouldn't be the whole truth.

"I can feel them move through me," I add, my voice quieter now.

It feels like a confession.

"There are these moments when I'm not so afraid.
When I'm not trying to control things.
When I can relax.
That's when I feel you the easiest."

I pause.

"There's a steadiness to you.
Like you don't get scared.
Like you don't cower or hide.
But it's deeper than that.
There's a certainty within you.
When I feel you, I feel it—a deep knowing
that everything is going to be okay.
That *I'm* going to be okay."

I take a breath.

"You feel closest when I feel hopeful.
In moments of awe and wonder, you are there.
When I'm hiking.
Traveling to new places.
Walking in the park.
Sitting in the sun.
Moments when I am present, when I stop fighting
with myself, I can feel this extra current
of energy. It feels bright
and happy in my chest."

I exhale slowly.

"That's what I know of you.
You are there when things are good.
You're comfortable in the good.
I'm not. I still struggle to trust it.
And that's why you come to me.
To remind me it won't always be this way.
To remind me that one day, I will be able to sit in it.
I will be able to sit in goodness without wanting to run."

I look at Future Me's face.

Her smirk is now a smile. She nods, the warmth in her eyes never wavering.

"You see me more than you realize."

She tilts her head slightly, considering all that I've said.

"You're right—I don't cower. I don't hide.
But that doesn't mean I don't feel fear.
I just don't let it drive anymore."

Her voice softens.

"I learned that fear isn't something to conquer or banish—
it's something to understand. To hold gently,
like a small, frightened bird."

She pauses. Lets the words settle.

"And you, my love, are already learning that.
That's why you feel me.
That's why you sense me in the stillness,
in the awe, in the wonder.
That's why I come to you."

Future Me leans forward slightly. Her voice soft but steady.

"You don't have to wait until 'one day' to sit in goodness.
You're already doing it, piece by piece.
You're already letting it touch you,
already letting it warm you.
You don't run as quickly as you used to."

She smiles. A quiet kind of pride in her expression.

"And that is how I know you're coming home to me."

I smile.

I know she's right. Even if I don't feel it yet.

"Okay, I have a question for you. What does it feel like to be you?"

She grins. A little sparkle flashes in her eyes.

"Now that is a good question."

She takes a moment, placing a hand over her heart, closing her eyes like she's feeling for the answer rather than thinking about it.

When she speaks, her voice is warm, certain.

"It feels free, expansive, like I have space—inside and out.
My chest isn't tight. My breath is easier.
I don't hold it as often.
There's no constant hum of self-doubt, no looping
thoughts about whether I've done enough,
been enough,
earned enough.
I know I am.
I don't have to prove it."

She opens her eyes and looks at me, her gaze steady.

"It feels like knowing I belong to myself.
In my own body.
In my own life."

Her voice softens.

"It feels like trust.
Not the blind kind, not the naïve kind.
The deep kind. The kind that's been tested
and earned. I trust myself.
And because of that, I trust life.

I trust my path.
I trust that even the hard moments, even the setbacks,
don't define me. They shape me.
And I don't have to brace for impact all the time."

She pauses, a playful glint in her eye.

"And, of course, it feels badass.
Because I know exactly who I am.
And I like who I am."

She leans back, her smile widening.

"That's what it feels like to be me."

I sit with her words for a moment. Let them wash over me like sunshine.

But then I feel it.

The familiar weight on my chest.

Doubt.

"It all sounds too good to be true.
I want to believe I can get where you are.
It just feels a million miles away, and I don't have a map.
I'm afraid of messing up.
Of disappointing you and every other version of myself.
I'm afraid of disappointing me."

Future Me tilts her head slightly, a knowing smile playing at her lips.

"Ah, there it is."

She leans forward, her gaze locking onto mine—not with judgment, not with impatience, but with something deeper.

Love.

Understanding.

"That feeling? That doubt creeping in?
That's just the old wiring talking.
The part of you that still believes you must earn
your way to me.
That there's some perfect path, some perfect version
of yourself you have to become first."

She shakes her head, her voice gentle but firm.

"There is no map, babe.
Because you're not following someone else's route—
you're making it as you go.
Step by step. Choice by choice.
And yeah, you're going to mess up.
You're going to take wrong turns.
You're going to get lost sometimes.
That's part of it."

Her expression softens.

"But you won't disappoint me.
You can't disappoint me.
Because every time you choose to try—every time
you choose you—you're already making your way
here."

She leans back, crossing her arms with a playful smirk.

"And between you and me? You're a lot closer than you think."

I like that idea. *I'm closer than I think.* Even if it doesn't feel that way.

"Future Me, what about Jason? Do you feel worthy of him? Because I still struggle sometimes."

Future Me's expression softens, and for a moment, I swear I see a flicker of something deep in her eyes—something tender that knows every doubt, every fear, every late-night question I've ever whispered into the dark.

She exhales, slow and steady, then leans forward, resting her chin on her hand.

"I don't just feel worthy of him," she says, her voice warm but unwavering.

"I know I am."

I shift in my seat, something inside me tightening.

"How?"

Future Me tilts her head, studying me.

"Because worthiness isn't about feeling like I deserve him.
It's about knowing I don't have to earn love.
That I don't have to shrink, or prove, or perform
to be loved well."

She smiles, amusement dancing in her eyes.

"Jason's love isn't a prize I won.
And I didn't trick him into loving me.
He chose me. Just like I chose him.
I stopped questioning why he loves me and started
focusing on how to let myself receive it."

My lips curl downward. Only for a second, but she catches it.

"You don't feel worthy of him because you're still
holding

onto the belief that love
is something you have to be good enough for.
But, babe...Jason's not loving some future, polished version of you.
He's loving you. Right now.
Mess and all."

She grins, shaking her head.

"And one day, you're going to let yourself believe that."

I try to let her words sink in, but I can still feel the resistance.

"I really hope you're right. I feel like you are. But I also know how I feel right now. I'm working on it, though."

I take a moment. Allow the resistance to move through me.

"What does it feel like to love yourself fully?
I can only do it in pieces, which is better than nothing at all,
but you seem to have done it. You seem to have figured out
how to move past your insecurities.
Past the conditioning.
Past your own expectations and unrealistic standards.
You've moved beyond it all.
So, what is it like?
What is it like to move through the world
as you?"

Future Me listens without interrupting, her eyes steady, thoughtful.

She lets the silence stretch, like she's allowing the weight of what I asked to settle between us.

Then, finally, she exhales, a small smile playing at her lips.

"It's not what you think," she says gently.

"Loving myself fully doesn't mean I never doubt.
It doesn't mean I never hear the old voices
or feel the old fears creeping in.
It doesn't mean I've moved beyond it all."

Her expression is soft but certain.

"It means I've learned to stay with myself through it.
To not abandon myself when the doubt creeps in.
To not shame myself when the fear lingers longer than I'd like."

Her eyes lock onto mine, grounding me.

"It means I've stopped treating love
like something I have to earn from myself.
It means I don't love myself in pieces anymore—
I love myself as a whole.
Not just the parts that are easy to love.
Not just the parts that feel strong or capable.
But the parts that are still healing.
The parts that are still afraid."

She tilts her head, considering me.

"You say you can only do it in pieces, but that's how it starts.
You hold the pieces. You learn to love them.
And then, one day, you realize
you're not holding separate pieces anymore—
you're holding you. And you're still here.
And you're still worthy."

She smiles now, something knowing in her expression.

"So, what does it feel like to move through the world as me?

"Steady.

Not because I never stumble, but because I trust myself
to stand back up.

"Expansive.
Not because I never feel small, but because I don't shrink
to make others comfortable.

"Free.
Not because I have no fears, but because I refuse
to let them cage me."

She pauses, then leans in, her voice softer now.

"But most of all, it feels like home."

She reaches across the space between us, her pinkie outstretched toward me.

"And you? You're on your way.
I pinkie promise you,
you're so much closer than you think."

My fingers twitch. I want to reach for her hand, but I don't.

I know what she's talking about.

Kind of.

I get glimmers of the feeling.

I have used it to move me forward.

Closer to her.

"So, we'll never be fully healed?
What you're saying is healing is ongoing?
It doesn't end, it expands?"

Future Me's smile deepens, like she's proud of me for getting there on my own. She nods.

"Exactly," she says, her voice warm.

"Healing isn't a finish line you cross.
It's not a checklist you complete.
It's an expansion.
A deepening.
A becoming."

She leans back slightly, her hands open in front of her like she's holding something delicate.

"It's like a horizon.
No matter how far you walk, it keeps stretching
ahead of you.
But that doesn't mean you're stuck.
It doesn't mean you're not making progress.
It just means there will always be more to explore,
more to uncover, more of you to meet."

Her eyes soften.

"But the difference is, you won't be afraid of it anymore.
You won't see healing as something you have to fix
about yourself.
You'll see it as a gift.
A lifelong unfolding.
You'll welcome it."

She tilts her head slightly, her voice taking on that light, playful spark.

"And if you think about it, isn't that better than being 'fully healed'?
Imagine if it just…ended.

If there was nothing left to grow into, nothing left
to expand toward.
That would be pretty fucking boring,
don't you think?"

She grins, and despite myself, I laugh. I shake my head.

"You're right."

She winks.

"I usually am."

Future Me's expression softens, and she leans in just slightly, like she's about to tell me a secret.

"That's why we are Everwoven." she says, her voice gentle but certain.

The word settles between us, like it's always been there, waiting for me to notice it.

Then, with a smirk, she adds,

"Also, because 'Megan' didn't have the same poetic ring to it."

She smiles, something steady in her expression.

"The life you're living, the healing you're doing—it's not linear.
It's not a straight path with a clear destination. It's threads.
Woven together, twisting and looping, some tangled, some smooth.
Each experience, each moment, each lesson—it all becomes
part of the fabric of you.
Every thread is a piece of your story.
Some you chose, some were given to you, some
you had to cut away.
But you are the one weaving it all together."

She gestures toward me

"You've been doing it all along.
You just didn't realize it.
Even in the moments you felt lost, even when
you thought you were unraveling—
you were still weaving.
You were still creating yourself."

She sits back slightly, giving me space to take it in.

I swallow, my throat tight.

"So, it doesn't matter that I'm not there yet?"

Future Me smiles, warm and knowing.

"You are there.
And you're still getting there.
Both can be true."

I think about what she's said, but it doesn't fully sit right.

"You're saying we are both the weaver and what's woven?
That every thread has its purpose?
I don't know how I feel about that.
The things that happened to me don't feel purposeful.
They just feel harmful most days.
Like I'm going to spend the rest of my life trying
to undo them.
Like I'm trying to unweave them from my life."

Future Me nods, her expression still gentle but now edged with something steadier—like she knew this was coming. Like she expected the
resistance.

"I hear you," she says.

"And I won't sit here and try to convince you
that everything that happened to you
was meant to happen.
I know how much you hate that idea.
And honestly? I agree with you.
Some things should never have happened.
Some threads were forced into your tapestry.
Some were woven with violence, with loss, with grief
so heavy it almost broke you."

She pauses, lets her words land before she continues.

"But healing isn't about unweaving those threads.
It's not about pulling them out like they were never there.
Because if you did that—if you truly unraveled every painful thing—
you wouldn't be left with some pure, untouched version of yourself.
You'd be left with holes. With gaps.
With missing pieces."

She leans in slightly, her eyes locked on mine.

"Healing isn't about undoing.
It's about reclaiming. It's about choosing
what to do with those threads.
Maybe you weave a new fabric from them.
Maybe you thread them through with gold, turn them
into something stronger.
Maybe you let them exist as they are,
but you stop letting them define the whole tapestry."

She exhales, tilting her head.

"You are Everwoven, not because everything was meant to happen,
but because you get to decide what it all means.

You are the weaver. You are the hands
holding the threads. And you get to create
something beautiful—not because of what happened,
but in spite of it."

She lets the words sit. Then, softer, she asks, *"Does that feel a little better?"*

I nod. My brow furrows.

"Kinda? Logically I understand what you're saying.
That we get to decide what the fabric of our lives looks like.
That we can decide whether we shape the fabric around the threads
of what happened to us, or if we just let them be a thread. A memory.
All of that makes sense. Logically.
I just don't know how to integrate it.
How to fully believe it.
How to make it part of me."

Future Me smiles, that soft knowing kind of smile, like she's heard this before.

Like she's been exactly where I am now.

"That's okay," she says.

"You don't have to know how to integrate it yet.
You don't have to force yourself to believe it overnight.
You think I got here by snapping my fingers and deciding
I was fully healed?"

She snorts, shaking her head.

"Come on now. You know us better than that."

Future Me leans forward. She watches me carefully, like she's been waiting for this.

"The truth is, integration isn't a moment. It's not a single choice.
It's a series of choices, again and again.
It's every time you remind yourself that you are more
than what happened to you.
Every time you catch yourself spiraling into self-blame
and gently pull yourself back.
Every time you soften
toward yourself instead of sharpening.
Every time you choose presence over panic,
love over fear, truth over the lies that trauma told you."

Her voice drops, steady and warm.

"And the most important part?
You don't have to rush it.
You don't have to force yourself to feel something just because
you think you should.
Let it come when it's ready.
Let it settle into your bones in its own time.
And in the meantime?"

She smiles, tilting her head.

"Just keep weaving.
Just keep moving.
Just keep choosing
yourself."

She watches me carefully, then adds, *"Doesn't that sound a little more doable?"*

I nod. "It does."

We sit in silence for a moment.

I know what I want to ask her. I'm just not sure I want to hear her answer.

I clear my throat. My stomach swirls.

I scratch at my thumbnails.

"Can I ask you something, and you'll tell me the real truth? Not what you think I want to hear?"

My voice is soft. Timid.

Future Me leans in, resting her elbows on her knees, her eyes steady and unwavering.

There's no hesitation in her expression—just warmth, just knowing.

"You know I will," she says, a small smirk tugging at the corner of her lips.

"I've never been here to tell you what you want to hear. I'm here to tell you what's real. What's true."

She tilts her head slightly, watching me, feeling me.

"So, go ahead, love. Ask me anything."

I rub my palms together. They're clammy from my nerves.

I take a deep breath.

Then another.

"What do you see when you look at me?"

Future Me exhales softly, like she's been waiting for this question.

Like she knew it would come.

She studies me for a long moment—not in the way people have before, not like she's trying to assess or judge or measure.

She's just seeing me.

Fully.

Completely.

Then, finally, she smiles.

"Oh, babe," she says, shaking her head just slightly, like she can't believe I don't already know.

"I see you."

She leans forward, her voice gentle but firm, steady as bedrock.

"I see the girl who carried the weight
of things no child should have to bear.
I see the teenager who folded herself into impossible
shapes just to survive.
I see the young woman who fought like hell
to carve out a different life,
even when she didn't know if she deserved one.
I see the woman who chose herself
and changed everything.
And I see you—now—right in front of me.
Sitting here, asking this question, looking for an answer
you already feel in your bones
but don't quite know how to trust yet."

She pauses, tilting her head slightly, her gaze unwavering.

"I see someone who has never, not once, stopped trying.
Even when you wanted to.
Even when you thought you had
Even when it felt impossible."

She leans back slightly, a soft, knowing smile on her lips.

"I see someone who is so close to stepping into herself.
Closer than she realizes.
Someone who has been unraveling the lies, untangling the knots,
making her way home—piece by piece, breath by breath."

Her voice dips into something softer, something deeper.

"I see magic, babe. The kind that never actually left you.
The kind you only forgot for a little while."

She smiles again, something playful flashing in her eyes.

"I see a woman who still thinks she's the student,
but, babe, she's already the teacher."

Future Me leans in now, closing the space between us just slightly.

"And do you want to know what else I see?"

I nod, my throat tight. Tears stream down my face.

"I see someone I am so damn proud of."

She pauses, letting the words settle, letting them land where they need to.

Then she grins.

"And between you and me?"

She winks, a spark of mischief in her eyes.

"I see someone who's gonna like being me."

After the Final Page

Writing *Everwoven* exposed me. To strangers, to my friends, to my family. There is much written on these pages that even my own sister didn't know. I kept my life, my struggles, my pain a secret from everyone. Especially those I loved and was terrified of losing. I didn't want to be a burden. To trauma dump. To be pitied.

I thought if my truth was revealed it would be all people would ever see—the sad girl who became a sad woman, destined to carry a sad story forever. Or worse, I'd be called 'resilient'—and goddamnit if I don't hate that fucking word.

I got great at deflecting when people would ask genuine questions about my life. My strategy was to give a quick superficial answer and then turn the conversation back to them. Maybe give a compliment, like asking about their shoes, even though I don't understand fashion and never had the mental space to learn.

I would ask real questions, genuine ones, but the answers felt irrelevant most of the time. It probably made me hard to talk to. I just wanted to keep the attention off of me. To keep me and my story hidden. Like I was a bank robber, only instead of stealing money, I was the one who had something stolen—my innocence, my self-worth, even my voice—and I didn't want to get caught with it missing.

But here's the thing: Like anyone else, I wanted to be seen. To be heard. To be understood. I wanted it so badly I would practice having conversations with Oprah while driving to work. Telling her my stories and imagining her looking at me, the way only Oprah can, and saying, "Damn, girl. That's some life you've led. That's some heavy shit to have to carry." Even in my imaginary commute chats with Oprah, I held some things back. Parts of me. The ones I thought were too big for the car. Or, too big for me.

That's why I played with the idea of writing a book but never actually did it. For years, I thought, *I should write a book*. But it was always a fleeting thought, because I knew what it would cost me. I would have to give up the armor I built around myself. The one that kept the world out. That kept me out, too.

I would have to come face-to face with the parts of me that I didn't even know how to contact. And even if I could make contact, what would I do with what I found? It never felt safe to excavate my story. To excavate my mind.

Until it did.

So, I thought I would share the messiness of it all. What writing my story brought forward for me, what insights I have gathered about myself since writing it, the most important ingredients in my healing cake—and the parts where I'm still eating shit.

So, let's get into it.

From a Hoodie to a Heartbeat

I can't tell you what inspired me to actually sit down and start writing, just that I was embarrassed as hell to even admit it. It took me an hour of hiding in my hoodie before I could even say the words out loud to Jason when he got home from work. It was a similar situation when I told Brittni, my therapist. I felt arrogant writing my story.

I felt ashamed.

Who the fuck am I to write a book?
Why would anybody even care about my life?
There are far worse stories out there. What right do I have to share mine?

These questions (and many others) swirled in my head, but even still, I wrote. It was all I wanted to do. I wrote for 10-12 hours daily for 30+ days straight. I didn't want to eat, sleep, or do anything other than write. I was more focused than I have ever been. More determined. A surge of electricity poured through me. Like there were live wires beneath my skin that wanted to spark with every key click. I felt like I was a conduit for something bigger than me. Like my story was demanding to be born and I was in labor.

I am not what most would call a writer. Sure, I've written papers for work and college, but nothing really outside of it. Hell, I audio journal instead of writing things down. I didn't know the first thing about writing a memoir, and I didn't bother to research it before starting. But, I've been collecting the words to my story for the last forty-three years, and when I finally let them out, they poured with ease.

I knew exactly how to write this book before I even started. It was like I'd written it before, over and over on the walls of my mind.

My paralyzing perfectionism disappeared. Unlike everything else in my life, I didn't walk into this feeling prepared. I didn't need to study the works of others to find my style. I didn't need to know the best practices. I didn't second-guess anything. Not my word choices. Not my structure. I just trusted what flowed. I knew the parts of me that needed to be heard were guiding this process, and I let them lead.

I probably broke every writing rule there is—but I didn't care. It wasn't about rules. It was about release.

Writing wasn't always easy. The urge to sanitize my truth, to make it more palatable, was always present. But I didn't shrink. I just wrote what was coming through.

When I read it back to myself, I went through a whirlwind of emotions. Embarrassment was chief among them.

Then shame.

Seeing my life looking back at me on the page brought some old wounds to the surface. Ones I know all too well.

I blamed myself for what I endured.
For how I handled it.
For not healing sooner.
For not being enough.

But the more I read, the more shame began to fade. And in its place, I felt pride.

I saw my strength, determination, and softness on full display.

I saw a little girl, a teenager, and a young woman who all endured more than they should have. Yet, even with every reason to be mad at the world, closed off, or uncaring, they each chose compassion. Maybe not for themselves, but for others. As I look at it now, that's the thing I'm the most proud of, and I have them to thank for it.

As I was writing, I knew I was doing something special, and I wanted to share it. But I was also terrified. I'd spent a lifetime perfecting how to be invisible in plain sight. To be interesting, but not memorable. To be engaging, but still isolated. That was my safety net. That was my armor. And sharing this book with the world meant putting it down.

The thoughts in my head went something like this,

I wonder if this book could ever be on Mel Robbins' podcast.

Fuck.
What would she ask me?
Would I have to set the scene more?
What if I can't remember all of the details? My memory has a lot of blank spots.

Would I have to explain the puppy mill? Would I be judged for going no-contact with Joy?

Would Mel judge the choices I made?
Am I allowed to call her Mel?
Would she think I'm a bad mom?
Would my son?

I hope I get to talk about Brandi. I hope someone asks.

Will people feel sorry for me? I don't do well with pity.

What do I say if someone compliments the book?
Is "thank you" enough?

What if they ask about my writing process?
Will they think I'm a fraud?
What if readers think I made it up?

What if no one reads it?

What if they do?

What if my friends read it?
What if my former students do?

Oh, Jesus Christ.
People are going to know me now.

Fuck.

It wasn't just a push-pull. It was a tug-of-war with my own body—visibility on one end, survival on the other. My stomach would drop every time I thought about questions I could be asked. It sometimes still does.

No one prepares you for how to step in front of the mirror when you've spent your life running from your own reflection. I was just learning how to see parts of myself and stay, so how could I expect random strangers to do the same?

Almost nightly, I had dreams about becoming visible to a crowd. I wouldn't call them nightmares, but I also wouldn't call them enjoyable either. The fear of my story being read, of my life being made public, was always in the back of my mind. I was both afraid and excited. With each finished chapter, the knot in my stomach became larger. I was pouring my soul onto the page and hoping not to be rejected by people I didn't even know. But now they knew me.

There were times my breath would become shallow and my body would literally begin to vibrate on the inside. The anxious anticipation of visibility was coursing through my nervous system. But I stayed grounded. I stayed (mostly) in control.

It took almost 350 hours of channeling my past selves, dictating their stories into my phone, writing, editing, and organizing for the first draft of *Everwoven* to be born. And when I got to that last line of my final chapter, I swear I could hear her heartbeat.

Baby Deer

So what now?

I'm about to have the very thing my soul has been aching for my entire life—to be seen.

And it's fucking terrifying and liberating at the same time.

I spend chunks of my day wondering how my life will change once this book is out into the world.

Will I walk differently?
Hold my head higher?
Be willing to take up space?

What changes when you're actually seen? When your story is known?

When you don't have to hide yourself from the world out of fear?

Will I believe in the rest of my dreams with the same ferocity as I have believed in Everwoven?

Who am I when I'm not hiding?

What will I do instead of bracing?

Will my mind be softer?

Will I just run the same script, even though I don't need to?

It's dizzying to think about.

That's the thing about visibility, and healing for that matter, that people don't talk about enough: when you make progress, it feels like going backward. You're exchanging the stability of the known—even if it isn't what you want— for the instability of something new.

It's like you're a baby deer having to learn to walk for the first time. Only in this situation, you're surrounded by other deer who can't understand why you're stumbling. Why your legs are wobbling. Why it feels challenging to do the thing that comes so easily to them.

It's part of why so many people give up on healing. Because the wobbles take time to steady, and during that time they face the judgement of others. So not only are they doing the scary thing of living in a new way, they're doing it with spectators pushing them to do it faster. To just be okay. So it makes sense why people return to old patterns— especially the high-functioning ones. At least then they know how to keep their legs from shaking.

But I don't want to go back. Not even when my legs shake. Not even when the old patterns feel easier. Because something in me is shifting—slowly, quietly, but undeniably. I've spent so long bracing, running, disappearing. Now, I'm trying something different. I'm trying to stay. To soften. To finally turn toward the parts of me I used to abandon.

I don't hate myself the way I used to. Not all the time, anyway. The voices are still there telling me the myriad of ways I am failing or a bad person. But they're quieter now. Less certain. I've started to question them instead of obeying them. To make room for other voices—kinder ones. Ones that sound like me. Or the version I'm still becoming.

I think of the past versions of myself, the ones who fought so hard to survive. Who screamed and shut down and acted out and held their breath for decades. I used to silence them. I used to act like their needs didn't matter. That they didn't matter.

Now, I'm trying to let them rest. I'm learning how to be the one who holds my past selves with care. Who tells them they don't have to keep watch anymore. That I'll stay. That I'll listen. That I've got us now. It's not perfect. But it's more peaceful.

Maybe that's what healing really is—when the war quiets, and you can finally hear your own heartbeat under all that noise.

When you can finally see yourself and say,

"Damn, girl. That's some life you've led. That's some heavy shit to have to carry. But look at you now. Still standing. Still soft. Still here."

www.ingramcontent.com/pod-product-compliance
Lightning Source LLC
Chambersburg PA
CBHW021701120626
46545CB00004B/1340